"If one of your goals for your child's education is for him to learn all about the 50 States, then you'll definitely want to [turn the pages of] this book! The author, Joel King, a homeschool dad has created something that will get both children and parents excited about learning the 50 states!

With 3 boys ages 5-14, I've seen plenty of curricula over the years, but this is truly the first that I've seen to take such a thorough approach to teaching the 50 states. It is just packed with information! My family absolutely loves the clip art and quick facts. I've never had a book that was such a complete resource. The Star-Spangled State Book gives the capital, the date the state entered the Union, the state's population and population ranking, the state's land area and land area ranking, the names of the 3 most populated cities, a picture of the state, the state flag, and then some other quick facts. That's a lot to learn, but this book will make it fun!

You won't find a more well-organized and thorough resource anywhere. Geography and history, facts and games, all work together to make this the best US geography curriculum on the market!"

Nancy Carter, The Old Schoolhouse® Magazine

"The Star-Spangled Workbook is designed to coincide with The Star-Spangled State Book. I am very impressed with this course! The author has thought of everything and included it in these two books!"

- **Heidi Strawser**, homeschool mom

Bonus Offer for Purchasers of the Star-Spangled State Book and Workbook Combo

Receive a free download of our Blackline Maps of American History: The Shaping of a Nation ($19.95 value) as our thank you for purchasing this product.

Your free ebook contains outline maps of all 50 states, along with 31 historical maps and a blank pull-out map of the United States.

Get your copy here:

www.knowledgequestmaps.com/dnldah.htm

Best Wishes,

Terri Johnson, VP Sales
Knowledge Quest, Inc.

THE
STAR-SPANGLED
WORKBOOK

Have Fun
Learning About
All 50 States

by Joel F. King

Published by BRAMLEY BOOKS
A Division of Knowledge Quest, Inc.
4210 Misty Glade
San Antonio, TX 78247
www.knowledgequestmaps.com

Cover Design by Cathi Stevenson

Illustration Credits

© 2006 Jupiterimages Corporation: front cover, back cover and almost every page in between!

Trademarks

The following trademarks were referred to in this book:
Wal-Mart® is a registered trademark of Wal-Mart Stores, Inc.
National Western® is a registered trademark of The Western Stock Show Association.
The Ford Motor Company® is a registered trademark of the Ford Motor Company.
General Motors® is a registered trademark of General Motors Corporation.
DaimlerChrysler® is a registered trademark of DaimlerChrysler AG Corporation Fed Rep Germany.
Snickers®, 3 Musketeers®, and Milky Way® are registered trademarks of Mars, Inc.

Acknowledgments

Special thanks to my wife and children for all of their help in making the idea for this book a reality. I
also want to thank Jupiterimages Corporation for their ability and willingness to make available many
of the images that have been used in this book.   Also, I want to thank Heidi Armstrong for her help in
editing this book.

Bibliography

Information for populations were calculated by the U.S. Census Bureau. The URL address for this information is as follows: http://www.census.gov/population/projections/state/stpjpop.txt. June 1, 2006

CONTENTS

A WORD TO THE INSTRUCTOR   4

U.S. MAP   5

OUTLINE OF LESSONS   6 - 9

1ST SEMESTER LESSONS   (LESSON 1.1 - LESSON 18.4)

2ND SEMESTER LESSONS   (LESSON 19.1 - LESSON 36.4)

ANSWER KEYS   241 - 257

STUDENT RECORD   258 - 259

A WORD TO THE INSTRUCTOR

Learning about our 50 unique states is a rewarding experience. However, before beginning, you may find it beneficial to read the following information.

1) To complete this course, students will need *The Star-Spangled STATE Book* and *The Star-Spangled WORKBOOK*.

2) This course is a 36-week program that is divided into two semesters. During the first four days of each week, students will complete one lesson plan a day. The fifth day can be used at your discretion.

3) During the first semester, students will learn about each state and complete a number of activites. They will also have to complete a number of quizzes and tests. A detailed lesson plan can be found on pages 6 - 9.

4) At the end of the first semester, students should be able to:

* IDENTIFY ALL THE STATES
* LOCATE THEM ON MAPS
* RECALL SOME BASIC STATE FACTS

5) During the second semester, students will expand upon what they have already learned. They will play games, take tests, and continue to study the states. By the end of the year, they should be able to:

* IDENTIFY ALL THE STATES
* LOCATE THEM ON MAPS
* RECALL EVEN MORE STATE FACTS
* KNOW THE STATE CAPITALS
* KNOW WHICH STATES BORDER WHICH

6) The lessons are in this book. They are in order and numbered for you.

7) Again, students only need to complete one lesson a day.

8) The answers to the quizzes and tests can be found in the back of this book.

9) Quizzes and exams are graded at your discretion. A page for recording the progress of a student has been included in this book.

THE 50 STATES

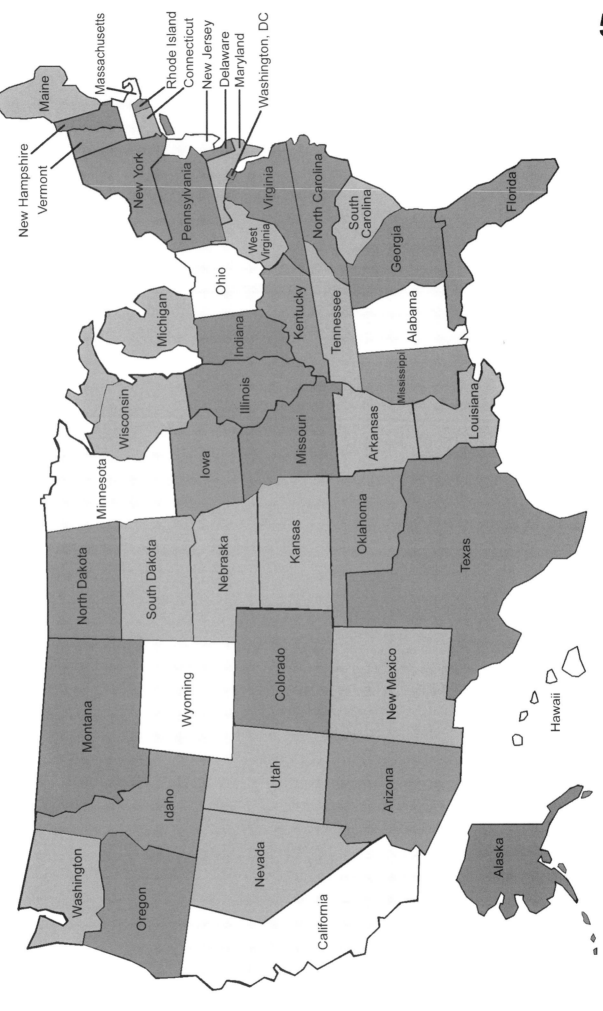

6

LESSON PLAN

WEEK #1
LESSON 1.1 THE UNITED STATES OF AMERICA -- OVERVIEW
LESSON 1.2 ALABAMA
LESSON 1.3 ALASKA
LESSON 1.4 ARIZONA and **QUIZ #1**

WEEK #2
LESSON 2.1 ARKANSAS
LESSON 2.2 CALIFORNIA
LESSON 2.3 COLORADO
LESSON 2.4 **QUIZ # 2**

WEEK #3
LESSON 3.1 CONNECTICUT
LESSON 3.2 DELAWARE
LESSON 3.3 FLORIDA
LESSON 3.4 **QUIZ #3**

WEEK #4
LESSON 4.1 GEORGIA
LESSON 4.2 HAWAII
LESSON 4.3 IDAHO
LESSON 4.4 **QUIZ #4**

WEEK #5
LESSON 5.1 ILLINOIS
LESSON 5.2 INDIANA
LESSON 5.3 IOWA
LESSON 5.4 **QUIZ #5**

WEEK #6
LESSON 6.1 KANSAS
LESSON 6.2 KENTUCKY
LESSON 6.3 LOUISIANA
LESSON 6.4 **QUIZ #6**

WEEK #7
LESSON 7.1 MAINE
LESSON 7.2 MARYLAND
LESSON 7.3 MASSACHUSETTS
LESSON 7.4 **QUIZ #7**

WEEK #8
LESSON 8.1 MICHIGAN
LESSON 8.2 MINNESOTA
LESSON 8.3 MISSISSIPPI
LESSON 8.4 **QUIZ #8**

WEEK #9
LESSON 9.1 MISSOURI
LESSON 9.2 MONTANA
LESSON 9.3 NEBRASKA
LESSON 9.4 **QUIZ #9**

LESSON PLAN

WEEK #10
LESSON 10.1 NEVADA
LESSON 10.2 NEW HAMPSHIRE
LESSON 10.3 NEW JERSEY
LESSON 10.4 **QUIZ #10**

WEEK #11
LESSON 11.1 NEW MEXICO
LESSON 11.2 NEW YORK
LESSON 11.3 NORTH CAROLINA
LESSON 11.4 **QUIZ #11**

WEEK #12
LESSON 12.1 NORTH DAKOTA
LESSON 12.2 OHIO
LESSON 12.3 OKLAHOMA
LESSON 12.4 **QUIZ #12**

WEEK #13
LESSON 13.1 OREGON
LESSON 13.2 PENNSYLVANIA
LESSON 13.3 RHODE ISLAND
LESSON 13.4 **QUIZ #13**

WEEK #14
LESSON 14.1 SOUTH CAROLINA
LESSON 14.2 SOUTH DAKOTA
LESSON 14.3 TENNESSEE
LESSON 14.4 **QUIZ #14**

WEEK #15
LESSON 15.1 TEXAS
LESSON 15.2 UTAH
LESSON 15.3 VERMONT
LESSON 15.4 **QUIZ #15**

WEEK #16
LESSON 16.1 VIRGINIA
LESSON 16.2 WASHINGTON
LESSON 16.3 WEST VIRGINIA
LESSON 16.4 **QUIZ #16**

WEEK #17
LESSON 17.1 WISCONSIN
LESSON 17.2 WYOMING
LESSON 17.3 WASHINGTON, D.C.
LESSON 17.4 **QUIZ #17**

WEEK #18
LESSON 18.1 REVIEW #1
LESSON 18.2 REVIEW #2
LESSON 18.3 REVIEW #3
LESSON 18.4 **SEMESTER EXAM #1**

LESSON PLAN

WEEK #19
LESSON 19.1 ALABAMA
LESSON 19.2 ALASKA
LESSON 19.3 ARIZONA
LESSON 19.4 **QUIZ #19**

WEEK #20
LESSON 20.1 ARKANSAS
LESSON 20.2 CALIFORNIA
LESSON 20.3 COLORADO
LESSON 20.4 **QUIZ #20**

WEEK #21
LESSON 21.1 CONNECTICUT
LESSON 21.2 DELAWARE
LESSON 21.3 FLORIDA
LESSON 21.4 **QUIZ #21**

WEEK #22
LESSON 22.1 GEORGIA
LESSON 22.2 HAWAII
LESSON 22.3 IDAHO
LESSON 22.4 **QUIZ #22**

WEEK #23
LESSON 23.1 ILLINOIS
LESSON 23.2 INDIANA
LESSON 23.3 IOWA
LESSON 23.4 **QUIZ #23**

WEEK #24
LESSON 24.1 KANSAS
LESSON 24.2 KENTUCKY
LESSON 24.3 LOUISIANA
LESSON 24.4 **QUIZ #24**

WEEK #25
LESSON 25.1 MAINE
LESSON 25.2 MARYLAND
LESSON 25.3 MASSACHUSETTS
LESSON 25.4 **QUIZ #25**

WEEK #26
LESSON 26.1 MICHIGAN
LESSON 26.2 MINNESOTA
LESSON 26.3 MISSISSIPPI
LESSON 26.4 **QUIZ #26**

WEEK #27
LESSON 27.1 MISSOURI
LESSON 27.2 MONTANA
LESSON 27.3 NEBRASKA
LESSON 27.4 **QUIZ #27**

WEEK #28
LESSON 28.1   NEVADA
LESSON 28.2   NEW HAMPSHIRE
LESSON 28.3   NEW JERSEY
LESSON 28.4   **QUIZ #28**

WEEK #29
LESSON 29.1   NEW MEXICO
LESSON 29.2   NEW YORK
LESSON 29.3   NORTH CAROLINA
LESSON 29.4   **QUIZ #29**

WEEK #30
LESSON 30.1   NORTH DAKOTA
LESSON 30.2   OHIO
LESSON 30.3   OKLAHOMA
LESSON 30.4   **QUIZ #30**

WEEK #31
LESSON 31.1   OREGON
LESSON 31.2   PENNSYLVANIA
LESSON 31.3   RHODE ISLAND
LESSON 31.4   **QUIZ #31**

WEEK #32
LESSON 32.1   SOUTH CAROLINA
LESSON 32.2   SOUTH DAKOTA
LESSON 32.3   TENNESSEE
LESSON 32.4   **QUIZ #32**

WEEK #33
LESSON 33.1   TEXAS
LESSON 33.2   UTAH
LESSON 33.3   VERMONT
LESSON 33.4   **QUIZ #33**

WEEK #34
LESSON 34.1   VIRGINIA
LESSON 34.2   WASHINGTON
LESSON 34.3   WEST VIRGINIA
LESSON 34.4   **QUIZ #34**

WEEK #35
LESSON 35.1   WISCONSIN
LESSON 35.2   WYOMING
LESSON 35.3   WASHINGTON, D.C.
LESSON 35.4   **QUIZ #35**

WEEK #36
LESSON 36.1   REVIEW #1
LESSON 36.2   REVIEW #2
LESSON 36.3   REVIEW #3
LESSON 36.4   **SEMESTER EXAM #2**

FIRST SEMESTER

LESSON PLANS
QUIZZES
TESTS

The United States of America

Welcome to your first day of United States Geography.

In this course, you'll learn about all fifty states! Fifty states? That's right! If you didn't already know that, then consider this the first thing you learned.

But there's so much more that you'll learn in this class. Here are a few:

* You'll learn what each state LOOKS like
* You'll learn how to find each state on the map
* You'll learn which states border one another
* You'll learn about important people and places
* And you'll learn about interesting events that you never knew about before.

BUT WHY IS THIS COURSE IMPORTANT?

Well, knowing more about your country can benefit you in many ways. First, you may want to move to another area of the country when you get older. Wouldn't it be helpful to know the wide variety of options that are out there? Second, one day, you may be sitting with your family to plan your next vacation. If you knew of a neat place to go, wouldn't you want to tell them about it? And third, a good understanding of your country will help you in other classes that you'll be taking in the future. With that in mind, it doesn't hurt to get a good headstart.

SOME THINGS THAT YOU WILL NEED.

In this course, you will need the following:
* This manual which contains all your lessons.
* The book entitled "The Star-Spangled State Book."
* Pencils (and some crayons, if you have them).

The following are optional:
* A map of the United States
* A globe

THE GAME PLAN

This class is a four-day-a-week class. That means you get a day off each week! (But don't get too excited. I'm sure your teacher has something else for you to do.)

Each day of class, you will need to complete a lesson from this workbook. The lessons are numbered at the top corner of each page, so it shouldn't be difficult to keep track of yourself.

Look at the top corner of this page. Do you see **LESSON 1.1**? Well, the first number stands for this course's <u>week</u> number, and the second number stands for this week's <u>day</u> number. Therefore, because today is the first week of your class (and it's also the first day of the week), you are doing Lesson 1.1. Tomorrow (the second day of your first week) is labeled Lesson 1.2.

Got it? Good!

Now, let's talk about the lessons. In a nutshell, there are three types of lessons. You have lessons where you will learn about the states; others where you'll takes quizzes; and some where you'll take tests. State lessons are the most common. Quizzes and tests usually come at the end of the week.

OK, LET'S BEGIN!

Now that you have a brief outline of this course, let's complete LESSON 1.1.

You live in the United States of America. OK, so it's a long name, but sometimes you'll see other words to describe this country. Shorter words and phrases like:

* *The United States*
* *The U.S.A.*
* *The U.S.*
* and *America*

Can you think of any other nicknames for your country? If you can, write them on these lines.

_____   _____   _____

Now, as we said before, the United States is divided into <u>fifty</u> areas that we call states. Forty-eight of these states are clustered together like pieces of a puzzle. But two states aren't. They are located in other places in the world.

Do you know the names of these two states? If you do, write their names here:

_____   _____

GO TO THE NEXT PAGE.
THIS LESSON IS NOT FINISHED YET.

The two states that are located in other parts of the world are Alaska and Hawaii! They are shown on this small map of the world.

Do you see them? Good.

And now that you have this map of the world in front of you, take a look at it and try to remember which parts make up the United States of America. Trust me, you'll be asked to find the United States on your first quiz! And when you're asked, don't forget about Alaska and Hawaii.

ACTIVITY: Do you have a globe handy? If you do, take a look at it and see if you can find Alaska, Hawaii, and the other 48 states.

Did you notice that Hawaii is made up of a cluster of small islands? That's right, there are many islands which help to form Hawaii. Did you notice anything else? Is Alaska way up near the North Pole? It certainly is! And the other 48 states? Are they all connected to one another? Yes, they are! And <u>the lines that seperate them from one another are called BORDERS.</u>

TURN THE PAGE. THERE IS MORE TO LEARN.

A NEW MAP. Here is another map of the United States. Take a look at it. Do you see any differences between the United States on this map and and the United States on the world map? Well, this map has <u>borders</u> to show you all the states. But there is more. The little guy standing at the bottom of the page will tell you about them.

Things you need to know:

Alaska and Hawaii (the islands) look out of place, don't they? Well, many U.S. maps look similar to this one. Do you know why they've been moved? Because Alaska and Hawaii are so far away from the other 48 states, someone came up with the cool idea to move them closer together and save space!

But that's not all they did. In order to save even more space, Alaska was shrunk and now appears smaller than California! Don't believe me? Well, take a look at a globe sometime and you'll see.

Oh, one more thing. Hawaii has been slightly enlarged so you wouldn't mistake it for some stray pencil marks.

Now that you have an overview of our country, take a rest. Your first lesson is over! See the stop sign? You will find one at the end of each lesson.

The State Pages

At the beginning of each day, turn to the correct lesson page in your *Star-Spangled WORKBOOK*. If the day's lesson is a quiz or test, then simply take the quiz or test; however, if the lesson is about a <u>specific</u> state, then you'll need to open your *Star-Spangled STATE Book* to the page of the state that's been identified. (For example, if you look at the next page, you'll notice that your first lesson is about Alabama. When you are ready to complete this lesson, you will need to turn to the *Alabama page* in your *Star-Spangled STATE Book*.)

Next, after finding the Alabama page in *The Star-Spangled STATE Book*, you'll need to read about the state. But be careful. If you don't understand the layout of the page, the information that you read may be confusing.

Let's take a look at a sample page from the *Star-Spangled STATE Book*. It's a copy of the *Alabama page*. Do you notice the black arrows and labels? These have been placed here to help you gain a better understanding of what you are studying. Do you see the state flag? Do you see the name of the state capital? Can you see Alabama's three largest cities? Birmingham is the largest; Montgomery is the next largest; and Mobile is the third largest city in the state.

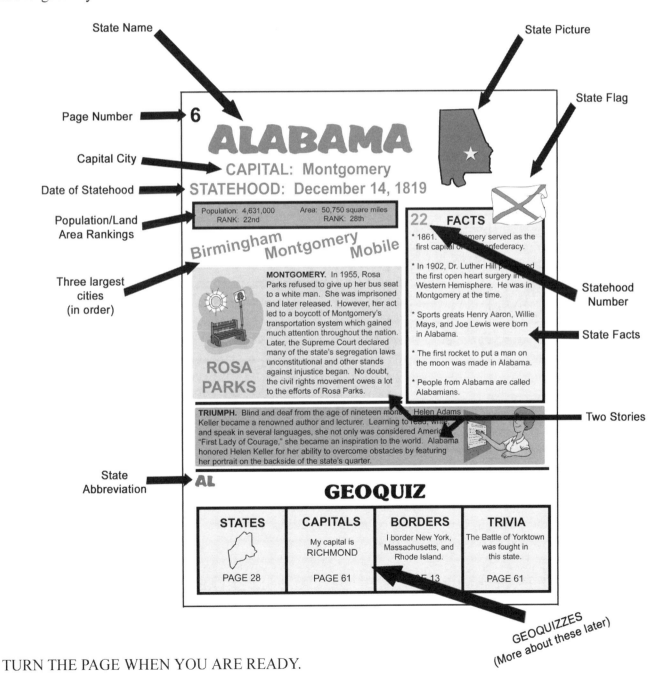

TURN THE PAGE WHEN YOU ARE READY.

NOTE: At the bottom of the *Alabama page* is a section entitled "GEOQUIZ." This section is actually a game that can be played, but you won't be taught how to play it until later. So, for now, you need to ignore this section and understand that it contains information that has <u>nothing</u> to do with your state lessons.

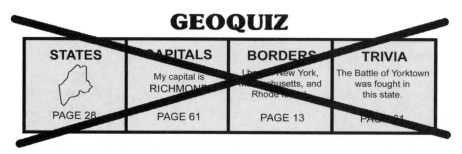

GEOQUIZ

STATES	CAPITALS	BORDERS	TRIVIA
	My capital is RICHMOND	New York, Massachusetts, and Rhode Island	The Battle of Yorktown was fought in this state.
PAGE 28	PAGE 61	PAGE 13	PAGE 61

REMEMBER: Ignore the GEOQUIZ section! Just study the information shown ABOVE it.

COMPLETING A LESSON. After you have finished learning about the day's state, you will need to come back to this WORKBOOK and complete your lesson. The lesson page for the state will have a front and back side. A sample is shown below.

FRONT   BACK

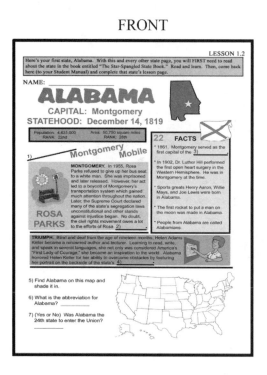

To complete a lesson, both sides of the page need to be filled out. Fortunately, these lessons may be completed <u>with</u> the aid of your *Star-Spangled STATE Book*. In other words, if you don't know the answer, you can look it up! Now that's not too difficult, is it? However, if you're taking a quiz or a test, you may <u>not</u> use any written materials to help you. You're on your own.

Remember: STATE PAGE = OPEN YOUR BOOK   QUIZ or TEST ≠ OPEN YOUR BOOK

OK, I think you're ready. Now turn the page to Alabama and begin. Remember, in order to complete this lesson, you will need to go the the *Alabama page* in *The Star-Spangled STATE Book*. Go over there, study, and then come back and complete your lesson. Good luck!

This lesson is about Alabama. Find the Alabama page in your *Star-Spangled STATE Book* and study it. Then, come back here and complete this lesson. Fill in all the blanks; complete all the tasks; and answer all the questions. In future state lessons, you will need to repeat these steps.

NAME: _____

ALABAMA

CAPITAL: Montgomery
STATEHOOD: December 14, 1819

Population: 4,631,000
RANK: 22nd

Area: 50,750 square miles
RANK: 28th

1) Montgomery Mobile

ROSA PARKS

MONTGOMERY. In 1955, Rosa Parks refused to give up her bus seat to a white man. She was imprisoned and later released. However, her act led to a boycott of Montgomery's transportation system which gained much attention throughout the nation. Later, the Supreme Court declared many of the state's segregation laws unconstitutional and other stands against injustice began. No doubt, the civil rights movement owes a lot to the efforts of Rosa 2)_____.

22 FACTS

* 1861. Montgomery served as the first capital of the 3)_____.

* In 1902, Dr. Luther Hill performed the first open heart surgery in the Western Hemisphere. He was in Montgomery at the time.

* Sports greats Henry Aaron, Willie Mays, and Joe Lewis were born in Alabama.

* The first rocket to put a man on the moon was made in Alabama.

* People from Alabama are called Alabamians.

TRIUMPH. Blind and deaf from the age of nineteen months, Helen Adams Keller became a renowned author and lecturer. Learning to read, write, and speak in several languages, she not only was considered America's "First Lady of Courage," she became an inspiration to the world. Alabama honored Helen Keller for her ability to overcome obstacles by featuring her portrait on the backside of the state's 4)_____.

5) Find Alabama on this map and shade it in.

6) What is the abbreviation for Alabama? _____

7) (Yes or No) Was Alabama the 24th state to enter the Union?

_____

II. What do you remember about Alabama? Use the space below.

Example: *Rosa Parks was from Alabama.*

_____

_____

_____

III. Write the definitions to these words in the spaces provided.

Boycott -- _____

_____

Obstacle -- _____

_____

IV. Draw a picture of Alabama.	**V. Connect the word to its correct picture.**
	ALABAMA
VI. Find Alabama on this map.	**VII. Unscramble these words.**
	LIEBOM _____
	SORA SPARK _____
	OJE SWILE _____
	SUB EATS _____

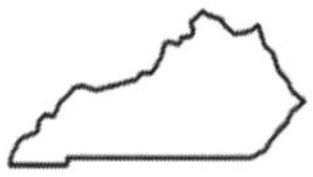

STOP

NAME: _____

Date: _____

ALASKA

CAPITAL: 1) _____

STATEHOOD: January 3, 1959

Population: 700,000   Area: 570,374 square miles
RANK: 47th   RANK: 1st

49 FACTS

* In 3) _____, the U.S. purchased Alaska from Russia. The price was just over 7 million dollars, or about 2 cents per acre. What a deal!

* Gold was discovered in Alaska by Joe Juneau in 1880. The state's capital is named in his honor.

* Alaska is called the Last Frontier State.

* By far, Alaska has more land than any other state.

* Alaska's Mount McKinley is the 4) _____ mountain in the U.S.

2) Juneau   Fairbanks

The Great Race. The Alaskan Iditarod is a dogsled race that covers over 1,150 miles. As participants make their way from Anchorage to Nome, they must cross frozen rivers, barren mountain ranges, dense forests, desolate tundras, and windy coastlines. It's no wonder that, after facing sub-zero temperatures and blinding winds for days at a time, some consider it a victory to just reach the finish line.

What time is it? Because of the natural wobble of the earth, the sun doesn't set in Barrow (America's northernmost city) between May 10th and August 2nd of each year! That's right, twenty-four hours of sunlight for more than 80 straight days. Then, come November, the sun doesn't rise above the horizon for sixty straight days on this city of nearly 5,000 people.

5. Find Alaska on this map and shade it in.

6. (Yes or No) The abbreviation for Alaska is AK? _____

7. In what year did Alaska become a state?
_____

ALASKA

II. What do you remember about Alaska? Use the space below.

_____

_____

_____

III. Write the definitions to these words in the spaces provided.

Tundra -- _____

_____

Frontier -- _____

_____

IV. Draw a picture of Alaska.	**V. Connect each word to its picture.**
	ALABAMA ALASKA
VI. Find Alaska on this map.	**VII. Unscramble these words.**
	UNAEJU _____ WARBOR _____ LUGHISTN _____ SNARKSED _____

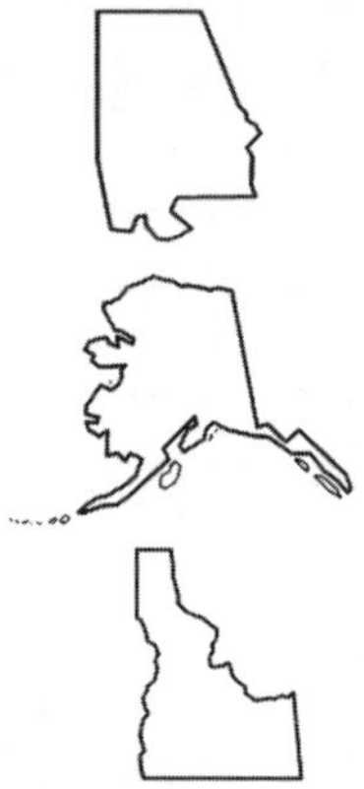

STOP

NAME: _____

LESSON 1.4

Date: _____

ARIZONA

CAPITAL: 1) _____

STATEHOOD: February 14, 1912

Population: 5,230,000	Area: 113,642 square miles
RANK: 20th	RANK: 6th

Phoenix   Tucson   Mesa

ONE OF SEVEN. The Grand Canyon is considered one of the seven natural wonders of the world. Stretching for over 277 miles, Arizona's magnificent ditch has an average width of 10 miles and an average depth of one mile. So, if you plan to visit the desert state, be careful of that first step!

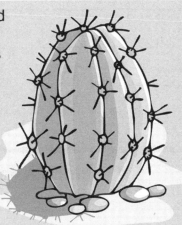

Note: In 1915, only 106,000 visitors saw the canyon. Today, more than four 2) _____ people visit each year.

48   FACTS

* Arizona is known as the Grand 3) _____ State.

* It's hard to believe, but the original London bridge is in Arizona! It was brought to the state from England and rebuilt, stone by stone.

* Arizona produces more copper than any other state.

* The tallest fountain in the world is believed to be located in Fountain Hills, Arizona.

* At least five flags have flown over the land that is now Arizona.

TOMBSTONE. On October 26th, 1881, Sheriff Wyatt Earp and his brothers, Morgan and Virgil, met their friend, Doc Holliday, on their way to the OK Corral. Here they confronted the Clanton and McLaury gang that had earlier threatened to kill the Earps. In the historic moments to follow, gunfire was exchanged and three men lay dead: Billy Clanton, Tom McLaury, and Frank McLaury. The fight lasted about 30 seconds.

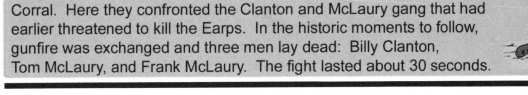

4. Find Arizona on this map and shade it in.

5. What is Arizona's population? _____

6. What is Arizona's abbreviation? _____

7. (True or False) Arizona was the 48th state to be admitted to the Union. _____

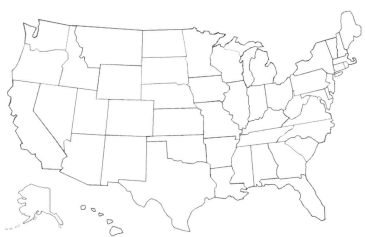

ARIZONA

II. What do you remember about Arizona? Use the space below.

_____

_____

_____

III. Write the definitions to these words in the spaces provided.

Grand -- _____

_____

Natural -- _____

_____

IV. Draw a picture of Arizona.

V. Connect each word to its picture.

ALABAMA

ALASKA

ARIZONA

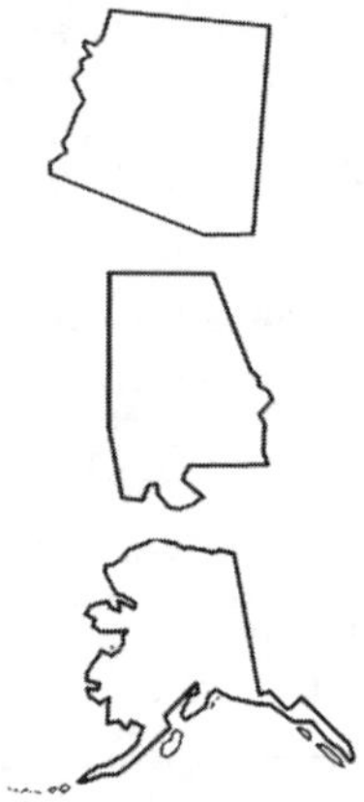

VI. Find Arizona on this map.

VII. Unscramble these words.

WATTY PARE   _____

ZONARIA   _____

CONUTS   _____

NOLOND GIDBER _____

Don't quit yet! You need to go to the next page and take a QUIZ!

NAME: _____

LESSON 1.4

Date: _____

QUIZ #1

1. Here is a map of the world. Color (or shade in) the area that is the United States of America.

"Don't forget about the island!"

---

2. Draw lines to connect each state name to its picture.

ARIZONA

ALASKA

ALABAMA

3. These three states are all scrambled up. Correctly spell them in the space provided.

ZONARIA   _____

SLAAKA   _____

AMABALA   _____

QUIZ #1

4. Three states are listed below. Color (or shade in) each of these states on the map. Then draw lines to connect each state name to its colored area.

Alaska   **Arizona**   **Alabama**

SECTION 5

A. The United States of America is divided into how many states? _____

B. What is a border? _____

C. I haven't mentioned this before, but there is a special name for the 48 states that are clustered together. Together, these 48 states are called the *Continental United States.* Now, with that in mind, which two states are NOT part of the *Continental United States?* _____ and

_____ .

NAME: _____

Date: _____

ARKANSAS

CAPITAL: 1) _____

STATEHOOD: June 15, 1836

Population: 2,750,000	Area: 52,075 square miles
RANK: 33rd	RANK: 27th

Little Rock Fort Smith Fayetteville

TWO TERMS. William Jefferson "Bill" Clinton, a native son of Arkansas, became the 42nd President of the United States in 1993. He served two terms and focused much of his domestic priorities on creating a universal healthcare system, improving education, restricting handgun sales, and strengthening America's environmental regulations. When he left office, his approval rating was a lofty 65%.

Bill 2) _____

25 FACTS

* Arkansas is called the 3) _____ State.

* In 1880, General Douglas MacArthur was born in Little Rock.

* Arkansas is home to Bentonville. Here, Sam Walton founded his Wal-Mart stores.

* Arkansas is famous for the Ozark National Forest and its many hot springs.

* A person from Arkansas is called an Arkansan.

NATURAL RESOURCES. Arkansas ranks first in the world in its production of bromine, an element that's useful in making sanitizers, dyes, and flameproofing agents. Also, over 80% of our nation's bauxite comes from Arkansas. So, what's bauxite? It's the ore from which our 4) _____ is made.

Al Aluminum

Atomic Number: 13
Atomic Mass: 26.98

5. Find Arkansas on this map and shade it in.

6. (True or False) The abbreviation of Arkansas is AK. _____

7. The population of Arkansas is just over 2.7 million. Where does this rank in comparison to the other states in the nation? 25th? 27th? Or 33rd? _____

ARKANSAS

II. What do you remember about Arkansas? Use the space below.

_____

_____

_____

III. Write the definitions to these words in the spaces provided.

Production -- _____

_____

Natural -- _____

_____

IV. Draw a picture of Arkansas.	V. Connect each word to its picture.
	ALASKA ARKANSAS ARIZONA

VI. Find Arkansas on this map.	VII. Unscramble these words.
	LLIB TONCLIN _____ LATURNA _____ LETLIT CORK _____ SASANRAK _____

STOP

CALIFORNIA

CAPITAL: 1) _____

STATEHOOD: September 9, 1850

Population: 34,441,000	Area: 155,973 square miles
RANK: 1st	RANK: 3rd

Los Angeles San Diego San Jose

GOLD RUSH. James Marshall discovered gold at Sutter's Mill on January 24th, 1848. By the end of that year, news spread of this event and California's Gold Rush began. Soon thereafter, the region's population swelled and California was "rushed" into statehood.

Note: Those who came to search for gold in California were called '49ers because 1849 saw huge population growth in the area.

31 FACTS

* San Francisco Bay is considered to be the world's largest landlocked harbor.

* If California was its own country, it would have the world's 5th largest economy!

* Some of California's giant redwood 2) _____ are over 2,000 years old.

*3) _____ Valley is considered the hottest and driest place in America.

* There are approximately 500,000 detectable seismic tremors in California each year!

A STICKY TREASURE. When the Portola Expedition passed through what is now California, Father Crespi wrote that a few members of their group saw "large marshes of a certain substance like pitch." Little did he know that the Rancho La Brea Tar Pits held the richest source of fossils in the world. So far, at least 60 species have been discovered in the tar springs, including saber-toothed cats, wolves, camels, bison, and mastodons.

4. Find California on this map and shade it in.

5. What is the name of the largest city in California? _____

6. (True or False) California has more land area than any other state. _____

7. (True or False) California has more people than any other state. _____

II. What do you remember about California? Use the space below.

_____

_____

_____

III. Write the definitions to these words in the spaces provided.

Rush --_____

_____

Giant --_____

_____

IV. Draw a picture of California.

V. Connect each word to its picture.

CALIFORNIA

ARIZONA

ARKANSAS

VI. Find California on this map.

VII. Unscramble these words.

LOGD SHUR   _____

FORINALICA   _____

SOL GELANES   _____

ANTGI WOODRED _____

STOP

NAME: _____

COLORADO

CAPITAL: 1) _____

STATEHOOD: August 1, 2) _____

Population: 4,468,000	Area: 103,729 square miles
RANK: 24th	RANK: 8th

Denver Colorado Springs Aurora

CATTLEMEN. The National Western Stock Show is regarded as the "Super Bowl of Cattle Shows." When it began in 1904, only four types of cattle competed, and most of these came from Colorado and neighboring states. But now the yearly event has grown. Not only do 19 breeds of cattle come from around the world to compete, there are also events for bison, goats, llamas, swine, sheep, and dogs.

38 FACTS

* Colorado is called the Centennial State because it was admitted to the Union on our nation's 100th birthday.

* More than 1/3 of Colorado's land is owned by the U.S. Federal Government.

* Colorado is home to the U.S. Air Force Academy.

* Colorado is split down the middle by the 3) _____ Mountains.

* Of all the states, Colorado has the highest average altitude.

PURPLE MOUNTAINS MAJESTY. In 1913, Katharine Lee Bates took a trip to Colorado Springs. While there, she visited Pike's Peak and said the following: "All the wonder of America seemed displayed there, with the sea-like expanse." Later, she penned the words to "America the Beautiful" and credited her visit to Colorado for the "purple mountains majesty" phrase.

4) Find Colorado on this map and fill it in.

5) What is Colorado's abbreviation? _____

6) Katharine Lee Bates wrote the words to what famous song? _____

7) (True or False) Of all the states, Colorado has the highest average altitude. _____

COLORADO

II. What do you remember about Colorado? Use the space below.

_____

_____

_____

III. Write the definitions to these words in the spaces provided.

Centennial -- _____

_____

Peak -- _____

_____

IV. Draw a picture of Colorado.

V. Connect each word to its picture.

COLORADO

CALIFORNIA

ARIZONA

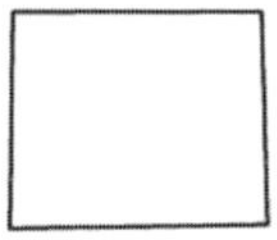

VI. Find Colorado on this map.

VII. Unscramble these words.

NEDVER _____

DOORCOLA _____

STAINMOUN _____

TUDEALTI _____

STOP

QUIZ #2

1. Three states are listed below. Color (or shade in) each of these states on the map. Then draw lines to connect each state name to its colored area.

California   Colorado   Arkansas

2. You should still remember these! Draw lines to connect each state name to its picture.

ARIZONA

ALASKA

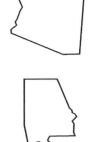

ALABAMA

3. These three states are all scrambled up. Correctly spell them in the space provided.

IFORCALINA _____

SLAAKA _____

SASARKAN _____

4. Correctly label each of the following state pictures. The last state begins with the letter <u>C</u>.

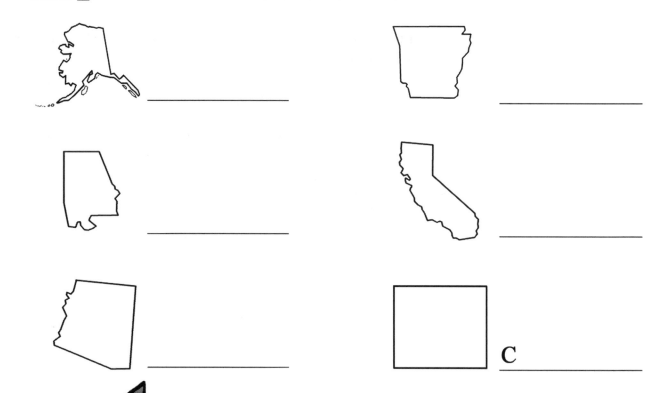

<u>CHECKPOINT!</u>

At this point you should be able to find SIX states on the map: **Alabama, Alaska, Arizona, Arkansas, California, and Colorado.**

Are you able to find them? I bet you can. But if you can't, don't worry. Just review these lessons until you're able. Between me and you, repetition is key!

Oh, and one more thing. Do you know what Arizona and California have in common? They border one another! Keep learning and in a few weeks, you might be able to close your eyes and name ALL the states that border California. And not just California, but any state!

Remember: U.S. Geography isn't hard; it's just a fifty-piece puzzle.

NAME: _____

CONNECTICUT

CAPITAL: 1) _____

STATEHOOD: January 9, 1788

Population: 3,317,000   Area: 4,845 square miles
RANK: 29th   RANK: 48th

Bridgeport   Hartford   New Haven

THE CONSTITUTION STATE.
No, it wasn't the first state
to ratify the Constitution; nor
did it host the signing. So
why is Connecticut called the
Constitution State? Well, over
100 years before we gained
our freedom from England,
little Connecticut had adopted
the Fundamental Orders.
These laws are so similar to the
American Constitution that the state has now become
known as the CONSTITUTION State. So, now you know.

5 FACTS

* Connecticut's motto is: "He who transplanted still sustains."

* The oldest newspaper that's still being printed is *The Hartford Courant*. It had its debut in 1764.

* In 1954, the first nuclear powered submarine was built in Connecticut. It was named the USS Nautilus.

* Connecticut's Mary Kies was the first woman to receive a U.S.
2) _____

* Noah Webster, author of America's first dictionary, was from South Killingly.

FAMOUS FACES. Connecticut was home to many famous
people: Ethan 3) _____ (the Revolutionary War hero),
John Brown (the abolitionist who sparked anti-slavery tensions),
Elias Howe (a famous inventor), Charles Goodyear (another
inventor), and Harriet Beecher Stowe (the author of Uncle
Tom's Cabin). Each of these has helped to shape America.

4) Find Connecticut on the map and shade it in.

5) What is the abbreviation of Connecticut?

_____

6) In what year did Connecticut become a
   state? _____

7) What is the name of Connecticut's most
   populated city? _____

CONNECTICUT

II. What do you remember about Connecticut? Use the space below.

_____

_____

_____

III. Write the definitions to these words in the spaces provided.

Ratify --_____

_____

Sustain --_____

_____

IV. Draw a picture of Connecticut.	V. Connect each word to its picture.
	CONNECTICUT COLORADO CALIFORNIA

VI. Find Connecticut on this map.	VII. Unscramble these words.
	FORDHART _____ RAMY SKIE _____ NAOH BEWSTER _____ THIFF TATES _____

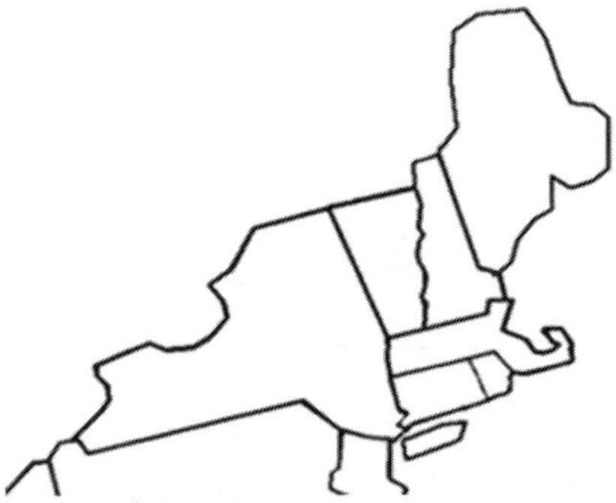

STOP

NAME: _____

DELAWARE

CAPITAL: 1) _____

STATEHOOD: December 7, 1787

Population: 800,000   Area: 1,955 square miles
RANK: 46th   RANK: 49th

Wilmington   Dover   Newark

1 FACTS

* Delaware is named in honor of Lord de la Warr. He was
3) _____ first governor.

* Speaking of names, the city of Milton is named in honor of John Milton, the famous English poet.

* Losing his entire fortune in the fight against slavery, Delaware's Thomas Garret helped more than 2,000 slaves escape to freedom.

* Horseshoe crabs can be seen along the Delaware shores in May. These creatures can go nearly a year without any food!

NUMBER 1. On December, 7th, 1787, the tiny state of Delaware had the distinction of leading our nation by becoming the first state to ratify the 2) _____.
That's right, the first state. Following its lead, the twelve other states existing at the time signed the document and the *United* States of America became official.

NUMBER 2. OK, so Delaware doesn't have the second MOST land; that honor goes to Texas. But little Delaware does have the second LEAST amount of land. With a mere 1,955 square miles of space, only Rhode Island is smaller. Still, despite its small area, Delaware's people have done much for this nation.

NOTE: Alaska, the largest state, could hold 291 states the size of Delaware.

4) Find tiny Delaware on this map and shade it in.

5) (Yes or No) DE is the abbreviation for Delaware. _____

6) On what date did Delaware become a state? _____

7) Who was Delaware named in honor of?

_____

II. What do you remember about Delaware? Use the space below.

_____

_____

_____

III. Write the definitions to these words in the spaces provided.

Distinction -- _____

_____

Governor -- _____

_____

IV. Draw a picture of Delaware	**V. Connect each word to its picture.**
	DELAWARE CONNECTICUT COLORADO
VI. Find Delaware on this map.	**VII. Unscramble these words.**
	FRIST TATES _____ ADEERLAW _____ ROVED _____ MALLS _____

FLORIDA

CAPITAL: 1) _____

STATEHOOD: March 3, 1845

Population: 16,279,000
RANK: 4th

Area: 53,997 square miles
RANK: 26th

Jacksonville Miami Tampa

3-2-1-BLASTOFF! Cape Canaveral is home to the John F. Kennedy Space Center. Since July 1st, 1962, NASA has used this facility to launch heroic astronauts and various craft into space. From Project Mercury to the space shuttles, hundreds of missions have started in Florida.

NOTE: Before President Kennedy's death, NASA's Cape Canaveral location was simply called the Launch Operations Center.

27 FACTS

* Florida is called the 2) _____ State.

* Saint Augustine is the oldest European settlement in North America.

* Of all the cities in America, Clearwater, Florida has the most lightning strikes each year.

* If you want to find the highest average temperature in the U.S., go to 3) _____ .

* Florida is home to Walt Disney World, a famous amusement park.

THE ORANGE OASIS. Florida is the orange capital of the world. Nearly 75% of U.S. oranges come from this state, and Florida produces almost 40% of the WORLD's orange juice supply! Surprisingly, however, the orange isn't native to Florida. In 1493, Christopher Columbus brought orange seeds to the Carolinas. Then, in 1513, explorer Ponce De Leon brought them to Florida.

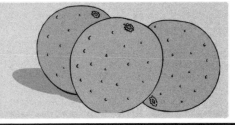

4) Find Florida on this map and shade it in.

5) What is Florida's abbreviation? _____

6) (True or False) Miami is Florida's most populated city? _____

7) NASA's space center is named after which American president? _____

FLORIDA

II. What do you remember about Florida? Use the space below.

_____

_____

_____

III. Write the definitions to these words in the spaces provided.

Astronaut --
_____

_____

Heroic --
_____

_____

IV. Draw a picture of Florida.

V. Connect each word to its picture.

FLORIDA

DELAWARE

CONNECTICUT

VI. Find Florida on this map.

VII. Unscramble these words.

GROANES _____

DRAFOIL _____

ENSHINUS _____

ROTANAUTS _____

STOP

NAME: _____

QUIZ #3

1. Three states are listed below. Color (or shade in) each of these states on the map. Then draw lines to connect each state name to its colored area.

Florida   Delaware   Connecticut

---

2. You should still remember these! Draw lines to connect each state name to its picture.

COLORADO

CALIFORNIA

ARKANSAS

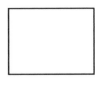

3. These three states are all scrambled up. Correctly spell them in the space provided.

a. ICUTCONNECT _____

b. AMALABA _____

c. LAREWADE _____

QUIZ #3

4. Correctly label these pictures.

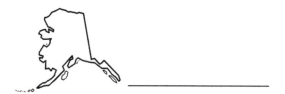 _____

 _____

 _____

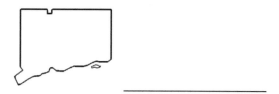 _____

 _____

 _____

5. Identify these states.

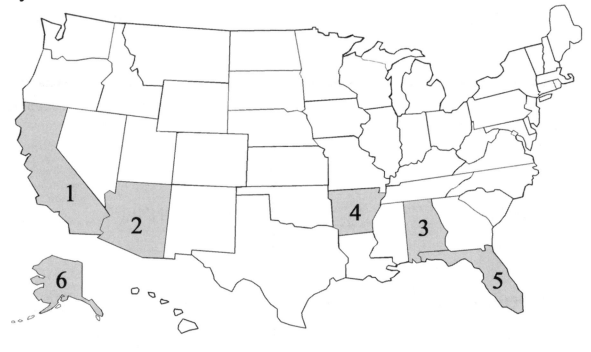

1._____   3. _____   5. _____

2._____   4. _____   6. _____

GEORGIA

CAPITAL: 1) _____

STATEHOOD: January 2, 1788

Population: 8,413,000	Area: 57,198 square miles
RANK: 9th	RANK: 21st

Atlanta   Augusta   Columbus

THE PEACH STATE. Georgia is quite famous for the quality and quantity of peaches it grows, but did you know the peach isn't native to Georgia? The fruit was first cultivated in China thousands of years ago. Later, it made its way along trading routes to Persia and Europe. Then, during the 16th and 17th centuries, Spanish ships carried the tasty fruit to the shores of America.

4   FACTS

* Georgia is named for England's King George II.

* Jimmy 2) _____ is from Georgia. He was the 39th President of the United States.

* Georgia has more land than any other state east of the Mississippi River.

* The famous pirate Edward Teach made a home on an island that's now part of Georgia. Who's Teach? He's better known as "Blackbeard."

* Georgia is called the Peach State and the Cracker State.

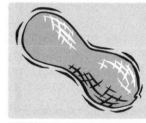

PEANUTS. Loved throughout the world, the peanut has become an important product for Georgia, where almost 40% of America's peanuts are grown. But like the peach, it isn't native to North America. Evidence suggests it originated in South America. So, how did it get to Georgia? Well, from South America, the Portuguese took the peanut to Africa, where it grew in popularity. From there, it was brought back across the 3) _____ Ocean to America.

4) Find Georgia on this map and shade it in.

5) What is the abbreviation for Georgia? _____

6) What delicious Georgia fruit is believed to have been first cultivated in China? _____

7) (True or False) The famous pirate Edward Teach, also known as Blackbeard, made a home on an island that's now part of Georgia. _____

II. What do you remember about Georgia? Use the space below.

_____

_____

_____

III. Write the definitions to these words in the spaces provided.

Delicious -- _____

_____

Cultivate -- _____

_____

IV. Draw a picture of Georgia.

V. Connect each word to its picture.

GEORGIA

FLORIDA

DELAWARE

VI. Find Georgia on this map.

VII. Unscramble these words.

AGEGORI _____

CHEAP _____

ANUPET _____

ALATTAN _____

STOP

HAWAII

CAPITAL: 1) _____

STATEHOOD: August 21, 1959

Population: 1,342,000   Area: 6,423 square miles
RANK: 40th   RANK: 47th

Honolulu   Hilo   Kailua

DECEMBER 7th. Hawaii is home to 2) _____ Harbor. During the morning hours of December 7th, 1941, combat planes from the Japanese fleet attacked our fleet while it was stationed there. Within ten minutes, five battleships were sunk or sinking, many American airplanes were destroyed, and over 2,400 Americans were dead. Sadly, what started as a peaceful Sunday morning turned into a call to arms and America's entry into the Second World War.

50   FACTS

* At one time, Hawaii was ruled by kings and queens. In fact, Hawaii's Iolani palace is the only royal palace in the U.S.

*3) _____ main islands help to form the state of Hawaii.

* Wow. Hawaii, not Florida, is the southernmost state.

* Unlike most states, the wind usually blows from east to west in Hawaii.

* Did you know that 1/3 of the world's pineapple supply comes from Hawaii?

THE LAST PIECE? In 1959, Hawaii became the last state to enter the Union. From thirteen to fifty, the United States has grown into one of the strongest nations in the world, and although there is currently no foreseeable 51st piece on the horizon, many are pushing to make Washington, D.C. a state. Another contender is Puerto Rico, an island territory off the coast of Florida. But, for now, the Aloha State maintains its status as the final piece to the American puzzle.

4) Find Hawaii on this map and shade it in.

5) (True or False) 1/3 of the world's apples come from Hawaii. _____

6) (True or False) Combat planes from the Japanese fleet attacked Pearl Harbor on December 7th, 1941. _____

7) Was Hawaii the 49th state to enter the Union? _____

HAWAII

II. What do you remember about Hawaii? Use the space below.

_____

_____

_____

III. Write the definitions to these words in the spaces provided.

Fleet -- _____

_____

Harbor -- _____

_____

IV. Draw a picture of Hawaii.	**V. Connect each word to its picture.** HAWAII GEORGIA FLORIDA 
VI. Find Hawaii on this map. 	**VII. Unscramble these words.** SLAT ATTES _____ IAWAHI _____ PRALE HARROB _____ BERNUM TIFFY _____

STOP

IDAHO

CAPITAL: 1) _____

STATEHOOD: July 3, 1890

Population: 1,480,000
RANK: 39th

Area: 82,751 square miles
RANK: 11th

Boise *Nampa* *Idaho Falls*

SCENIC WONDERLAND. Idaho is an outdoor adventure. Alpine lakes, mountain peaks, canyons, and waterfalls are just some of the splendor the state has to offer. Also, because of the variety of landscapes, you can visit rolling hills, hot springs, and even high country deserts and sand dunes! And the wildlife? It's abundant. Without a doubt, Idaho offers plenty to those who enjoy the outdoors.

43 FACTS

* Idaho is known as the Gem State because of the many precious stones that can be found there.

* Like most western states, Idaho had its 2) _____ and silver rushes. Today, a number of "ghost" towns remain. They include: Silver City, Yankee Fork, and Gold Dredge.

* The world's largest man-made geyser can be found in Soda Springs.

* Beware! In Idaho, it's against the law for one citizen to give another a box of candy weighing more than 50 pounds!

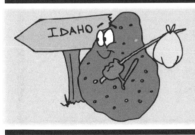

IDAHO AND THE POTATO. When many think of Idaho, they think of the potato, because over 30% of American potatoes come from the state. But few know the potato isn't native to Idaho. Many scientists believe the spud had its beginnings in South America and was brought to North America long before Columbus arrived; however, it wasn't until 1836 that it found a home in Idaho!

3) Find Idaho on this map and shade it in.

4) (True or False) Idaho's abbreviation is ID.
_____

5) According to this page, how many people live in Idaho? _____

6) Approximately what percent of American potatoes come from Idaho? _____

7) In what year did Idaho become a state?
_____

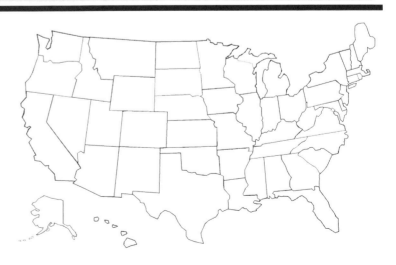

IDAHO

II. What do you remember about Idaho? Use the space below.

_____

_____

_____

III. Write the definitions to these words in the spaces provided.

Gem --
_____

_____

Precious --
_____

_____

IV. Draw a picture of Idaho.

V. Connect each word to its picture.

IDAHO

HAWAII

GEORGIA

VI. Find Idaho on this map.

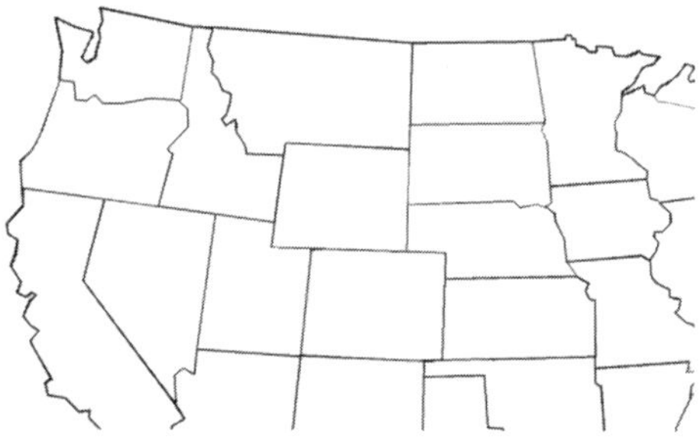

VII. Unscramble these words.

AHODI   _____

MEG TATES   _____

TOPTAO   _____

CREPIOUS   _____

STOP

QUIZ #4

1. Three states are listed below. Color (or shade in) each of these states on the map. Then draw lines to connect each state name to its colored area.

Hawaii   Idaho   Georgia

---

2. You should still remember these! Draw lines to connect each state name to its picture.

ARIZONA

ALABAMA

DELAWARE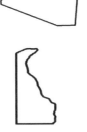

---

3. These three states are all scrambled up. Correctly spell them in the space provided.

AWARDELE _____

ADIFLOR _____

ICUTCONNECT _____

QUIZ #4

Correctly label these six state pictures.

_____

_____

_____

_____

_____

_____

Identify these states.

1 _____   2 _____   3 _____

4 _____   5 _____   6 _____

ILLINOIS

CAPITAL: 1) _____

STATEHOOD: December 3, 1818

Population: 12,266,000	Area: 55,593 square miles
RANK: 6th	RANK: 24th

2) _____

Aurora   Rockford

THE GIPPER. Illinois is the birthplace of Ronald Wilson Reagan, the 40th President of the United States. Born in Tampico, Reagan moved to California, where he became an actor. Later, he stepped onto the political stage and was elected California's governor. President Reagan served two terms in the White House and is credited with winning the Cold War.

21 FACTS

* In 1871, the Great Chicago 3) _____ killed about 200 people, destroyed 17,500 buildings, and left nearly 90,000 people homeless.

* Illinois was the first state to ratify the 4) _____ Amendment to the Constitution. This law abolished slavery.

* The world's first skyscraper was built in Chicago, not New York.

* If you're looking for a good book, come to Chicago. Its public library has over two million books, making it one of the world's largest.

A BUSY, BUSY PLACE. Chicago's O'Hare International Airport is the busiest airport in the world. Even when you consider its large number of connections to multiple locations throughout the world, it's still hard to imagine that over 190,000 travelers pass through its terminals on a normal day.

5) Find Illinois on this map and shade it in.

6) Who was the 40th President of the United States? _____

7) In what city was the world's first skyscraper built? _____

II. What do you remember about Illinois? Use the space below.

_____

_____

_____

III. Write the definitions to these words in the spaces provided.

Airport -- _____

_____

Library -- _____

_____

IV. Draw a picture of Illinois.

V. Connect each word to its picture.

ILLINOIS

IDAHO

HAWAII

VI. FInd Illinois on this map.

VII. Unscramble these words.

INOSILLI _____

ICAGOCH _____

RIFE _____

TROPAIR _____

STOP

NAME: _____

INDIANA

CAPITAL: 1) _____

STATEHOOD: December 11, 1816

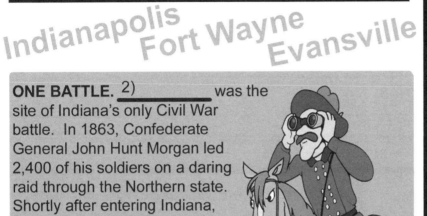

Population: 6,215,000 RANK: 15th	Area: 35,870 square miles RANK: 38th

Indianapolis Fort Wayne Evansville

19 FACTS

* Indiana is called the Hoosier State.

* In addition to being the site of Indiana's only Civil War battle, Corydon also served as the state's first 3) _____ .

* The first Europeans to settle in what is now Indiana were not the English. They were French.

* Southern Indiana holds some of the richest deposits of limestone in the world! New York's Empire State Building, the U.S. Treasury, and fourteen state capitol buildings are built from Indiana's treasure.

ONE BATTLE. 2) _____ was the site of Indiana's only Civil War battle. In 1863, Confederate General John Hunt Morgan led 2,400 of his soldiers on a daring raid through the Northern state. Shortly after entering Indiana, the Rebels met Harrison County's small force of 450 men. After a few volleys, Morgan accepted their surrender. He met no further resistance until after he entered Ohio.

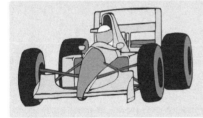

THE INDIANAPOLIS 500. In 1911, the first long-distance auto race was held in the city of Indianapolis. Since then, this yearly event has attracted more fans, faster cars, and more money for the winner. The winner of the first race averaged 75 miles per hour and received a $14,000 prize. Today, speeds average around 167 miles per hour and the winner receives more than 1.2 million dollars.

4) Find Indiana on this map and shade it in.

5) (True or False) Indiana's abbreviation is IN. _____

6) What famous automobile race is held in Indiana each year? _____

7) In what year did Indiana become a state? _____

INDIANA

II. What do you remember about Indiana? Use the space below.

_____

_____

_____

III. Write the definitions to these words in the spaces provided.

Limestone --

_____

_____

Battle --

_____

_____

IV. Draw a picture of Indiana.	**V. Connect each word to its picture.**
	INDIANA **ILLINOIS** **IDAHO**
VI. Find Indiana on this map.	**VII. Unscramble these words.**
	HIROOSE TATES _____ ANAINDI _____ CRYNOOD _____ SLIMETONE _____

NAME: _____

Date: _____

IOWA

CAPITAL: 1) _____

STATEHOOD: December 28, 1846

Population: 2,941,000   Area: 55,875 square miles
RANK: 30th   RANK: 23rd

Des Moines Cedar Rapids Davenport

CORN. There are believed to be over 3,500 uses for corn. From aspirin to diapers, from food to automobile fuel, it seems new ways of using this important crop are being discovered every day.

NOTE: Of the nearly 10 billion bushels of corn grown yearly in the U.S., roughly 57% is fed to livestock, 19% is exported to other countries, and 12% is used in ethanol fuel. America's five biggest customers for corn are: Japan, Mexico, Taiwan, South Korea, and Egypt.

29 FACTS

* Herbert 2) _____, the 31st President of the United States, was from Iowa. He was the first president to be born west of the Mississippi River.

* John Wayne, the famous actor, was born in Winterset. Many remember him as "The Duke."

* Glenn Miller, orchestra leader and trombonist, was born in Clarinda.

* The 3) _____ River forms Iowa's eastern border and the Missouri River forms its western border.

THE BIG BREADBASKET. It has been estimated that each farmer in Iowa produces enough food to feed 279 people. Now that's what I call productive! Corn, soybeans, and hogs are just some of the sources of nutrition that come from the Hawkeye State. So, the next time you visit the grocery store, remember that a small part of Iowa may be in your buggy.

4) Find Iowa on this map and shade it in.

5) (True or False) The abbreviation for Iowa is IA. _____

6) What famous actor was born in Iowa?
_____

7) What famous orchestra leader was born in Iowa? _____

IOWA

II. What do you remember about Iowa? Use the space below.

_____

_____

_____

III. Write the definitions to these words in the spaces provided.

Crop -- _____

_____

Productive -- _____

_____

IV. Draw a picture of Iowa.	**V. Connect each word to its picture.** **IOWA** **INDIANA** **ILLINOIS**
VI. Find Iowa on this map. 	**VII. Unscramble these words.** REMARF _____ SCROP _____ YOS SNABE _____ AWOI _____

STOP

QUIZ #5

1. Three states are listed below. Color (or shade in) each of these states on the map. Then draw lines to connect each state name to its colored area.

Iowa   Illinois   Indiana

---

2. See if you can remember these! Draw lines to connect each state name to its picture.

COLORADO

IDAHO

ARIZONA

---

3. These three states are all scrambled up. Correctly spell them in the space provided.

HOIDA   _____

OWIA   _____

ANADINI   _____

QUIZ #5

LESSON 5.4

Correctly label these six state pictures. The last one begins with the letter <u>C</u>.

 _____

 _____

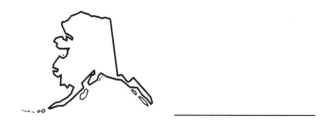 _____

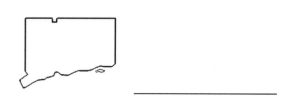 _____

 _____

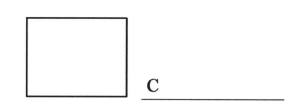 C _____

Identify these states.

1 _____

2 _____

3 _____

4 _____

5 _____

6 _____

STOP

NAME: _____

KANSAS

CAPITAL: 1) _____

STATEHOOD: January 29, 1861

Population: 2,761,000   Area: 81,823 square miles
RANK: 32nd   RANK: 13th

Wichita
Overland Park
Kansas City

WATCH OUT! Tornadoes are storms with rapidly rotating winds that form funnel clouds. Unfortunately, many of these touch the ground, causing much damage with their nearly 300 mile per hour winds. As you may recall in the movie "The Wizard of Oz," a Kansas girl by the name of Dorothy was even whisked away by one. But is Kansas the most active tornado state? No, it isn't! On average, three other states receive more. And in relation to land size, Kansas ranks a distant fifth.

34 FACTS

* Dodge City is proclaimed to be the 2) _____ city in America.

* The geographic center of the 48 contiguous states is in Kansas.

* The first woman mayor in the U.S. was from Kansas. In 1887, Susan Salter was elected to office in Argonia.

* Kansas is important to U.S. land surveyors. When they're outside checking the positions of properties, they're really checking their positions in relation to Kansas' Meades Ranch, our nation's benchmark.

AMELIA EARHART. The most famous woman in aviation history is from Kansas. In 1932, Amelia Earhart became the first woman (and only the second person) to fly solo across the Atlantic Ocean. Then, in 1935, she became the first person to fly solo from Hawaii to California. However, her career was cut short in 1937 when she perished in the 3) _____ Ocean after failing to find a small island that was to serve as her landing site.

4) Find Kansas on this map and shade it in.

5) (Yes or No) KA is the abbreviation for Kansas. _____

6) In what year was Susan Salter elected Argonia's mayor? _____

7) What is the name of the most populated city in Kansas? _____

KANSAS

II. What do you remember about Kansas? Use the space below.

_____

_____

_____

III. Write the definitions to these words in the spaces provided.

Solo -- _____

_____

Aviation -- _____

_____

IV. Draw a picture of Kansas.

V. Connect each word to its picture.

KANSAS

IOWA

INDIANA

VI. Find Kansas on this map.

VII. Unscramble these words.

ROTANDO _____

DINWY _____

ASKSAN _____

POKEAT _____

STOP

KENTUCKY

CAPITAL: 1) _____

STATEHOOD: June 1, 1792

| Population: 4,098,000 | Area: 39,732 square miles |
| RANK: 25th | RANK: 36th |

Lexington Owensboro

2) _____

FAMOUS KENTUCKIAN. Abraham Lincoln was born in Kentucky in 1809. After moving with his family to Illinois, the young man took it upon himself to grow in knowledge. Working on farms, splitting rails, and tending to a store were only some of the duties Lincoln performed. However, his passion soon turned to politics, where he was able to represent the Republican Party, win the 1860 Presidential Election, and lead America through the most trying period of its history, the 4) _____ War.

ABRAHAM

3) _____

15 FACTS

* Jefferson Davis was from Kentucky. He served as the Confederate president during the Civil War.

* During the War of 1812, over half of all the Americans killed were from Kentucky, the Bluegrass State.

* Kentucky is home to Fort Knox. Much of the nation's gold is held here.

* More than 100 Kentuckians have been governors of OTHER states!

* The Kentucky Derby is the oldest yearly horse race in the country.

NATURAL WONDER. Mammoth Cave is true to its name. It's a whopper! Even with over 365 miles of charted passageways, it's still believed that there are hundreds of miles left to be discovered. Nearly two million people visit the huge cavern each year to see "rooms" large enough to hold office buildings, underground rivers, and creatures that can seldom be seen anywhere else in the world.

5) Find Kentucky on this map and shade it in.

6) What is the abbreviation for Kentucky?

_____

7) (True or False) More than 100 Kentuckians have been governors of OTHER states.

_____

II. What do you remember about Kentucky? Use the space below.

_____

_____

_____

III. Write the definitions to these words in the spaces provided.

Fort -- _____

_____

Mammoth -- _____

_____

IV. Draw a picture of Kentucky.	**V. Connect each word to its picture.**
	KENTUCKY KANSAS IOWA
VI. Find Kentucky on this map.	**VII. Unscramble these words.** THAMMOM VACE _____ TROF NOXK _____ LOGD _____ TUCKENKY _____

NAME: _____

LOUISIANA

LESSON 6.3

Date: _____

CAPITAL: 1) _____

STATEHOOD: April 30, 1812

Population: 4,535,000	Area: 43,566 square miles
RANK: 23rd	RANK: 33rd

2) _____ Baton Rouge / Shreveport

THEY WOULD NOT BOW. A large number of 3) _____ live in Louisiana, but do you know what makes these people special? Why, they're the descendants of the Acadians who were driven out of Canada during the 1700s. OK, and who were the Acadians? The Acadians were the first FRENCH settlers in what are now the Canadian provinces of Nova Scotia, New Brunswick, and Prince Edward Island. They were forced from Canada when they refused to pledge allegiance to the King of *England*.

18 FACTS

* Louisiana was named in honor of France's King Louis XIV.

* During the 4) _____ War, twenty major battles took place in Louisiana during a two-year span.

* The Mississippi River meets the Gulf of Mexico in Louisiana.

* The word "bayou" is French. It signifies a slow-moving river.

* Jazz, a form of music, had its birth in Louisiana. In the 1920s and 1930s, it reached its height of popularity.

FAT TUESDAY. What would you do the day before forty days of fasting was to begin? Well, they throw a party in New Orleans! Mardi Gras (meaning "Fat Tuesday" in French) is a festival that has become a yearly event in Louisiana. Coming the day before the Christian observance of Lent, the celebration is still growing in popularity, even after 300 years.

5) Find Louisiana on this map and shade it in.

6) What is Louisiana's abbreviation? _____

7) Who was Louisiana named in honor of? _____

LOUISIANA

II. What do you remember about Louisiana? Use the space below.

_____

_____

_____

III. Write the definitions to these words in the spaces provided.

Gulf -- _____

_____

Jazz -- _____

_____

IV. Draw a picture of Louisiana.	V. Connect each word to its picture.
	LOUISIANA KENTUCKY KANSAS

VI. Find Louisiana on this map.	VII. Unscramble these words.
	GINK ISOUL _____ CUMIS _____ WEN ASORLEN _____ NOTAB OUGER _____

STOP

QUIZ #6

1. Three states are listed below. Color (or shade in) each of these states on the map. Then draw lines to connect each state name to its colored area.

Kansas   Louisiana   Kentucky

2. See if you can remember these! Draw lines to connect each state name to its picture.

INDIANA

IOWA

ILLINOIS

3. Here are a few more to try! Draw lines to connect each state name to its picture.

CONNECTICUT

IDAHO

GEORGIA

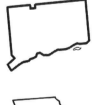

QUIZ #6

Identify these states.

1 _____ 2 _____ 3 _____

4 _____ 5 _____ 6 _____

Identify these states.

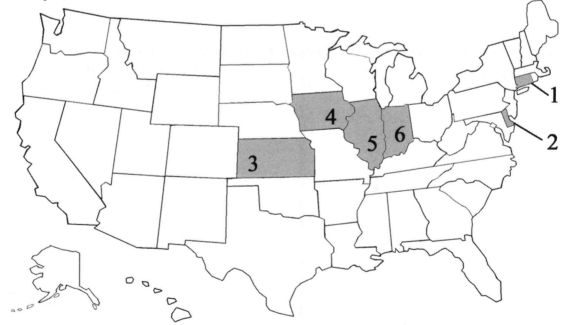

1 _____ 2 _____ 3 _____

4 _____ 5 _____ 6 _____

MAINE

CAPITAL: 1) _____

STATEHOOD: March 15, 1820

Population: 1,285,000	Area: 30,865 square miles
RANK: 41st	RANK: 39th

Portland   Lewiston   Bangor

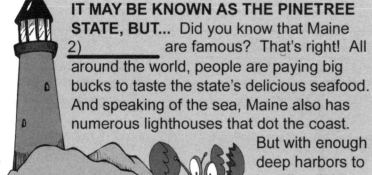

IT MAY BE KNOWN AS THE PINETREE STATE, BUT... Did you know that Maine 2) _____ are famous? That's right! All around the world, people are paying big bucks to taste the state's delicious seafood. And speaking of the sea, Maine also has numerous lighthouses that dot the coast. But with enough deep harbors to handle all the navies of the world, they are necessary.

23   FACTS

* Eastport is America's easternmost city. It's said to be the first place in the U.S. to see the morning sun.

* Maine's Acadia National Park is the second most visited national park in America.

* Poet Henry Wadsworth Longfellow was from Maine.

* In 1623, America's first sawmill was built near York, Maine.

* After the War of 3) _____, Eastport remained in British hands. Their rule didn't end until 1818.

BEAUTIFUL LAND. Nearly 90% of America's toothpicks come from Maine's timber, and the state's production of blueberries is second to none. In fact, about 99% of all our blueberries come from Maine! That's right, 99%! And then there's the snow. With its alpine mountains, the state is a great place for those who love the outdoors.

4) Find Maine on this map and shade it in.

5) (True or False) The abbreviation for Maine is ME. _____

6) What is Maine's largest city? _____

7) What is the name of America's easternmost city? _____

MAINE

II. What do you remember about Maine? Use the space below.

_____

_____

_____

III. Write the definitions to these words in the spaces provided.

Timber -- _____

_____

Coast -- _____

_____

IV. Draw a picture of Maine.	V. Connect each word to its picture.
	MAINE **LOUISIANA** **KENTUCKY**
VI. Find Maine on this map.	**VII. Unscramble these words.** ANIME _____ BERTIM _____ STERLOBS _____ NOWS _____

NAME: _____

MARYLAND

CAPITAL: 1) _____

STATEHOOD: April 28, 1788

Population: 5,467,000	Area: 9,755 square miles
RANK: 19th	RANK: 42nd

Baltimore Gaithersburg Rockville

OH SAY, CAN YOU SEE?
During the War of 1812, Washington, D.C. was captured by the British, and the city of Baltimore was next. Through the Maryland harbor, British warships made their approach, but Fort McHenry stood in their way.

From the deck of a ship, Francis Scott Key, a patriot, watched the fort being bombarded. Through the night, he stood, and when he saw America's flag still waving in the morning, he penned the words to our national anthem.

7 FACTS

* Did you know that Maryland gave up some of its land to help form Washington, D.C.? Virginia was the only other state to lend a hand.

* Clara 2) _____ was the founder of the American Red Cross. At one time, her home in Glen Echo served as the organization's headquarters.

* Other famous Marylanders include: Vice President Spiro Agnew, author Upton Sinclair, baseball great Babe Ruth, and abolitionists Harriet Tubman and Frederick Douglas.

ANNAPOLIS. Once called the Athens of America, the city of Annapolis is a national treasure: the Maryland city once served as our nation's capital; since 1845 it has served as the home of the U.S. Naval Academy; four signers of the Declaration of Independence lived there; it boasts more surviving colonial buildings than any other city; and it was where the Treaty of Paris was ratified in 1784 to end the Revolutionary War.

3) Find Maryland on the map and shade it in.

4) What is Maryland's abbreviation? _____

5) (Yes or No) Did Maryland give up some of its land to help form Washington, D.C.? _____

6) Who penned the words to the American national anthem? _____

7) Annapolis was once called the _____ of America.

MARYLAND

II. What do you remember about Maryland? Use the space below.

_____

_____

_____

III. Write the definitions to these words in the spaces provided.

Bombard -- _____

_____

Patriot -- _____

_____

IV. Draw a picture of Maryland.	**V. Connect each word to its picture.**
	MARYLAND MAINE LOUISIANA
VI. Find Maryland on this map.	**VII. Unscramble these words.** MOREIBALT _____ TORF CHEMRYN _____ RAW FO 1218 _____ PARIOTT _____

STOP

NAME: _____

Date: _____

MASSACHUSETTS

CAPITAL: 1) _____

STATEHOOD: February 6, 1788

Population: 6,310,000	Area: 7,838 square miles
RANK: 13th	RANK: 45th

Boston Worcester Springfield

6 FACTS

* The first subway system in the U.S. was built in Boston in 1897.

* The USS Constitution (or Old Ironsides) is berthed at Charleston Navy Yard. This famous ship served our nation during the Revolutionary War.

* The Boston Tea Party took place in Massachusetts shortly before the Revolutionary War began.

* In 1692, the infamous 3) _____ Witchcraft Trials led to the deaths of twenty citizens.

THE PILGRIMS. On December 21st, 1620, a group of English Puritans came to America aboard the 2) _____. Their intent was to escape religious persecution, create a new settlement, and practice religion the way they felt was right. The famous place where they landed is known as Plymouth Rock.

THANKSGIVING

HEROES OF THE REVOLUTION. Minutemen played a vital role in the American Revolution, especially in Massachusetts. Armed, mobile, and always ready for action, these brave men were usually the first to arrive for battle.

4) Find Massachusetts on the map and shade it in.

5) (True or False) Minutemen played a vital role in the Civil War. _____

6) What is the name of the largest city in Massachusetts? _____

7) According to this page, what is the population of Massachusetts? _____

MASSACHUSETTS

II. What do you remember about Massachusetts? Use the space below.

_____

_____

_____

III. Write the definitions to these words in the spaces provided.

Persecution -- _____

_____

Pilgrim -- _____

_____

IV. Draw a picture of Massachusetts.	**V. Connect each word to its picture.** **MASSACHUSETTS** **MARYLAND** **MAINE**
VI. Find Massachusetts on this map.	**VII. Unscramble these words.** MOUTHPLY _____ GRIMPILS _____ EAT TRAPY _____ MUTEINNEM _____

STOP

QUIZ #7

1. Three states are listed below. Color (or shade in) each of these states on the map. Then draw lines to connect each state name to its colored area.

Maryland   Massachusetts   Maine

---

2. See if you can remember these! Draw lines to connect each state name to its picture.

CONNECTICUT

KANSAS

ALABAMA

---

3. Here are a few more to try! Draw lines to connect each state name to its picture.

INDIANA

ILLINOIS

KENTUCKY

QUIZ #7

Identify these states.

1 _____   2 _____   3 _____

4 _____   5 _____   6 _____

Identify these states.

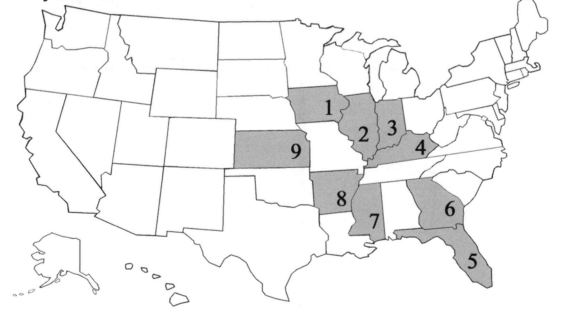

1 _____   2 _____   3 _____

4 _____   5 _____   6 _____

7 _____   8 _____   9 _____

STOP

NAME: _____

MICHIGAN

CAPITAL: 1) _____

STATEHOOD: January 26, 1837

Population: 9,763,000   Area: 56,809 square miles
RANK: 8th   RANK: 22nd

26 FACTS

2) _____ Grand Rapids   Warren

THE WOLVERINE STATE.
Michigan is the Wolverine State, but what exactly is a wolverine? Well, the wolverine is a member of Mustelidae family (animals such as skunks, otters, and weasels). Though small in size, the powerfully-built animal is suited for winter survival and is fearless. As a matter of fact, the wolverine won't hesitate to attack sheep, deer, or even small bears! Sadly, the wolverine is on the endangered species list and can no longer be found in Michigan.

* The University of Michigan was the first university to be established in any state.

* Gerald R. Ford, the 38th President of the United States, was raised in Grand Rapids.

* The Detroit Zoo was the first zoo to offer cageless exhibits.

* Boats, boats, and more boats. Michigan has more boats registered in it than any other state.

* The Detroit-Windsor tunnel was the first tunnel to connect two countries.

CAR CAPITAL OF THE WORLD. Yes, the city of Detroit and the surrounding area have helped turn Michigan into the largest manufacturer of cars. The Ford Motor Company, General Motors, and DaimlerChrysler call Michigan their home. Together, these three have placed millions of vehicles on the road.

3) Find Michigan on this map and shade it in.

4) (True or False) Michigan's abbreviation is MI. _____

5) What city's zoo was the first to offer cageless exhibits? _____

6) (Yes or No) Is Michigan called the Hawkeye State? _____

7) What U.S. President was raised in Grand Rapids, Michigan? _____

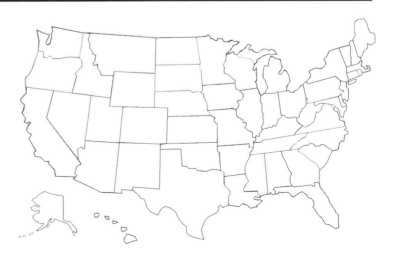

MICHIGAN

II. What do you remember about Michigan? Use the space below.

_____

_____

_____

III. Write the definitions to these words in the spaces provided.

Endangered -- _____

_____

Species -- _____

_____

IV. Draw a picture of Michigan.

V. Connect each word to its picture.

MICHIGAN

MASSACHUSETTS

MARYLAND

VI. Find Michigan on this map.

VII. Unscramble these words.

GNACHIMI _____

ROITDET _____

SCAR _____

WINEVOLER _____

STOP

MINNESOTA

CAPITAL: 1) _____

STATEHOOD: May 11, 1858

Population: 5,005,000	Area: 79,617 square miles
RANK: 21st	RANK: 14th

Minneapolis Saint Paul Rochester

FISHING, ANYONE? With more than 90,000 miles of shoreline, Minnesota has more than California, Florida, and Hawaii combined. Couple that with the excellent fishing, and it's no wonder the state boasts having one recreational boat for every six of its citizens. But beware of meeting someone at Mud Lake, Rice Lake, or Long Lake. With over 10,000 bodies of water, these common names have been used over 100 times each!

32   FACTS

* Minnesota is known as the Land of 10,000 Lakes, but that is a low estimate.

* Minnesota is home to the Mayo Clinic. This teaching facility is known throughout the world for its expertise in the medical field.

* America's first 2) _____ marrow transplant took place in Minnesota.

* Have you ever eaten a Snickers, 3 Musketeers, or Milky Way bar? Frank C. Mars, the inventor of these tasty treats, was from Minnesota.

DID THE 3) _____ **REACH AMERICA BEFORE COLUMBUS?** An archeological site in Minnesota suggests that they might have. In 1898, the Kensington Runestone was discovered near Alexandria, Minnesota. Its carvings tell the journey of a band of Vikings that reached North America in 1362, over 100 years before Columbus. Also, evidence in eastern Canada suggests that Leif Eirikson entered the Gulf of Saint Lawrence.

4) Find Minnesota on this map and shade it in.

5) With over 5 million people, Minnesota is ranked _____ st in the U.S.

6) What is the name of Minnesota's largest city? _____

7) (True or False) Minnesota's abbreviation is MI. _____

MINNESOTA

II. What do you remember about Minnesota? Use the space below.

_____

_____

_____

III. Write the definitions to these words in the spaces provided.

Evidence --_____

_____

Archeology --_____

_____

IV. Draw a picture of Minnesota.	V. Connect each word to its picture.
	MINNESOTA MICHIGAN MASSACHUSETTS
VI. Find Minnesota on this map.	**VII. Unscramble these words.** KINGVIK _____ IFGNISH _____ 01,000 KALES _____ ANESTOMIN _____

STOP

NAME: _____

MISSISSIPPI

CAPITAL: 1) _____

STATEHOOD: December 10, 1817

Population: 2,908,000   Area: 46,614 square miles
RANK: 31st   RANK: 31st

Jackson   Gulfport   Biloxi

THE KING. 2) _____ Presley, also known as the King of Rock and Roll, was born in Tupelo, Mississippi on January 8th, 1935. For more than two decades, the singer set and broke many records for both record sales and concert attendance. Some of his music includes: "Love Me Tender," "Jailhouse Rock," and "Kentucky Rain." Elvis passed away in 1977, but millions of fans from around the world continue to buy his music.

20   FACTS

* In 1902, President 3) _____ Roosevelt refused to shoot a captured bear while he was visiting Mississippi. His kind act led to the creation of the cuddly "Teddy" bear, a bedroom favorite.

* 59,000 of the 78,000 Mississippians who fought in the Civil War were either wounded or killed in action.

* Captain Isaac Ross was from Mississippi. Who is he? In 1834, Captain Ross freed his slaves and made arrangements to send them to Africa. There, they founded the country of Liberia.

OLD MAN RIVER. Mississippi shares its name with America's longest river, the Mississippi River. Forming much of the state's western border, the mighty river has played an important role in the development of the country. In the 1800s, riverboats transported people and goods along the river, turning many towns into lively cities with strong economies. Mark Twain's "The Adventures of Huckleberry Finn" captures this spirit.

4) Find Mississippi on this map and shade it in.

5) (True or False) Mississippi's abbreviation is MS. _____

6) Mark Twain wrote "The Adventures of Huckleberry _____."

7) In what year did Mississippi become a state? _____

MISSISSIPPI

II. What do you remember about Mississippi? Use the space below.

_____

_____

_____

III. Write the definitions to these words in the spaces provided.

Arrangement -- _____

_____

Economy -- _____

_____

IV. Draw a picture of Mississippi.	**V. Connect each word to its picture.** **MISSISSIPPI** **MINNESOTA** **MICHIGAN**
VI. Find Mississippi on this map.	**VII. Unscramble these words.** "DYDET ARBE" _____ ASIAC SORS _____ IALIBER _____ REVIR _____

STOP

QUIZ #8

1. Three states are listed below. Color (or shade in) each of these states on the map. Then draw lines to connect each state name to its colored area.

| Minnesota | Michigan | Mississippi |

---

2. See if you can remember these! Draw lines to connect each state name to its picture.

MASSACHUSETTS

ALABAMA

MISSISSIPPI

3. Here are a few more to try! Draw lines to connect each state name to its picture.

IOWA

LOUISIANA

MAINE

QUIZ #8

Identify these states.

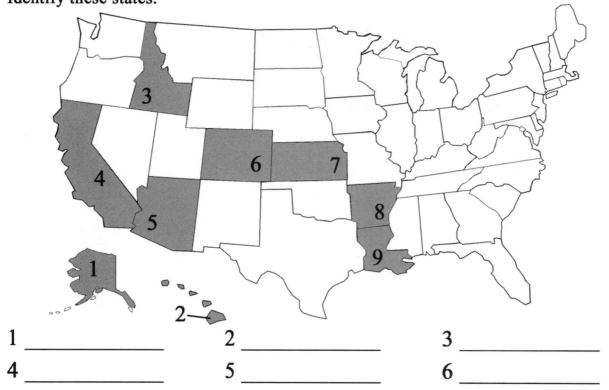

1 _____ 2 _____ 3 _____

4 _____ 5 _____ 6 _____

7 _____ 8 _____ 9 _____

Identify these states.

1 _____ 2 _____ 3 _____

4 _____ 5 _____ 6 _____

7 _____ 8 _____ 9 _____

MISSOURI

CAPITAL: 1) _____

STATEHOOD: August 10, 1821

Population: 5,718,000   Area: 68,898 square miles
RANK: 17th   RANK: 18th

Kansas City Saint Louis Springfield

PENNSYLVANIA OF THE WEST?
Missouri is called the "Show Me State," but some still refer to it as the "Pennsylvania of the West." Why? Well, while Missouri's economy developed with its rise in population, many noticed the similarities between its growth and that of Pennsylvania. Mining was of great importance and, likewise, manufacturing within the state was on the rise.

24 FACTS

* Missouri, like Tennessee, borders 2) _____ states. No other states border as many.

* President Harry S. Truman was born in Lamar. He was president at the close of the Second World 3) _____.

* Saint Louis is home to the famous Gateway Arch. During the 1960s, this monument was built to honor the spirit of the early pioneers.

* Saint Louis. In 1912, John Berry made the first successful parachute jump from a moving airplane.

THE GROUND SHOOK. The most powerful earthquake to shake America didn't occur in California; it was in New Madrid, Missouri. At two o'clock in the morning on December 16th, 1811, the quake started. Huge cracks split the ground; the waters of the Mississippi River rose and fell so forcefully that giant waves swept upstream to Louisville, Kentucky; and church bells were made to ring in Boston, Massachusetts, which was over 1,000 miles away!

4) Find Missouri on this map and shade it in.

5) (True or False) The abbreviation for Missouri is MO. _____

6) Saint Louis is home to the famous _____ Arch.

7) (True or False) Missouri was the 24th state to be admitted to the Union. _____

MISSOURI

II. What do you remember about Missouri? Use the space below.

_____

_____

_____

III. Write the definitions to these words in the spaces provided.

Tremor -- _____

_____

Pioneer -- _____

_____

IV. Draw a picture of Missouri.

V. Connect each word to its picture.

MISSOURI

MISSISSIPPI

MINNESOTA

VI. Find Missouri on this map.

VII. Unscramble these words.

I DERBOR 8 _____

AQUEETHARK _____

WEN DRIMAD _____

SIMISOUR _____

STOP

MONTANA

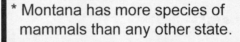

CAPITAL: 1) _____

STATEHOOD: November 8, 1889

Population: 1,006,000
RANK: 44th

Area: 145,556 square miles
RANK: 4th

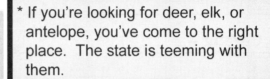

41 FACTS

* Montana has more species of mammals than any other state.

* If you're looking for deer, elk, or antelope, you've come to the right place. The state is teeming with them.

* Yellowstone National Park was our country's 2) _____ national park. The park covers areas of Montana, Wyoming, and Idaho.

* Lots of land and few people. With only six people per square mile, Montana offers plenty of elbow room.

Billings Missoula Great Falls

THE TREASURE STATE.
Montana is home to some of America's richest deposits of rare minerals. When gold was discovered in 1862, many settlers came to the area, hoping to strike it rich. In time, they discovered copper, silver, sapphires, opals, and platinum. Today, many of the areas where mining occurred have become ghost towns, but Montana's resources still touch all our lives.

YELLOW HAIR. Montana is home to the 3) _____ Bighorn Battlefield. Here, in 1876, Lt. Colonel George Custer and the Seventh Cavalry fell in battle to a group of Sioux and Cheyenne Indians that left their reservations, outraged by the continued intrusions of gold seekers into their sacred lands in the Black Hills. In the end, the Union Cavalry lost over 260 men and the Indian alliance lost nearly 200.

4) Find Montana on this map and shade it in.

5) (True or False) Montana's abbreviation is MT. _____

6) What is the name of Montana's largest city? _____

7) (True or False) In land area, Montana ranks 44th. _____

MONTANA

II. What do you remember about Montana? Use the space below.

_____

_____

_____

III. Write the definitions to these words in the spaces provided.

Mineral -- _____

_____

Cavalry -- _____

_____

IV. Draw a picture of Montana.	**V. Connect each word to its picture.** **MONTANA** **MISSOURI** **MISSISSIPPI**
VI. Find Montana on this map.	**VII. Unscramble these words.** **LETLIT HIBGORN** _____ **RALSMINE** _____ **MANTONA** _____ **BELOW MORO** _____

STOP

NEBRASKA

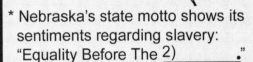

CAPITAL: 1) _____

STATEHOOD: March 1, 1867

Population: 1,761,000   Area: 75,898 square miles
RANK: 38th   RANK: 15th

Omaha   Lincoln   Bellevue

MOO. Although Nebraska ranks 38th in population, its cattle industry is one of the top in the nation. Here are a few facts: Nebraska ranks 1st in its number of live animal and beef exports; 2nd in the amount of revenues it receives from the sales of cattle and calves; and 3rd in its total number of cattle. With an estimated 6.35 MILLION head, Nebraska holds almost 7% of our nation's herd!

37 FACTS

* Nebraska's state motto shows its sentiments regarding slavery: "Equality Before The 2) _____."

* Most states have two houses of legislature: a house and a senate. However, Nebraska only has one.

* Weeping Water is home to the nation's largest limestone deposit.

* During World War II, over 40% of our nation's ammunition was made in Hastings, Nebraska.

* President Gerald R.3) _____ was born in Nebraska.

THE CORNHUSKER STATE. As its nickname implies, Nebraska is a large producer of corn, but this wasn't always the case. At one time, Nebraska was called the "Great American Desert." Thankfully, those days are gone and the state has been transformed into a farmer's paradise through the use of progressive farming techniques and irrigation. In fact, with over 80,000 wells to draw water from, Nebraska has become the 3rd largest corn-producing state.

4) Find Nebraska on this map and shade it in.

5) What is Nebraska's abbreviation? _____

6) (True or False) Nebraska is called the Bluegrass State. _____

7) What is the name of Nebraska's largest city? _____

NEBRASKA

II. What do you remember about Nebraska? Use the space below.

_____

_____

_____

III. Write the definitions to these words in the spaces provided.

Motto --
_____

_____

Irrigation --
_____

_____

IV. Draw a picture of Nebraska.

V. Connect each word to its picture.

NEBRASKA

MONTANA

MISSOURI

VI. Find Nebraska on this map.

VII. Unscramble these words.

BENASARK _____

RINGFAM _____

RIGIRATION _____

HUSKCORNER _____

STOP

QUIZ #9

1. Three states are listed below. Color (or shade in) each of these states on the map. Then draw lines to connect each state name to its colored area.

Montana   Nebraska   Missouri

2. Identify these states.

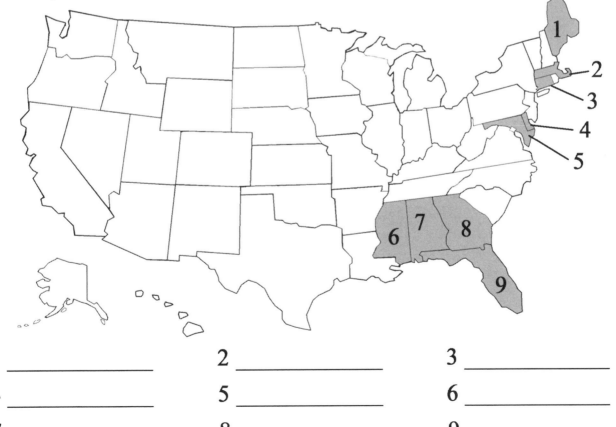

1 _____   2 _____   3 _____

4 _____   5 _____   6 _____

7 _____   8 _____   9 _____

QUIZ #9

Identify these states.

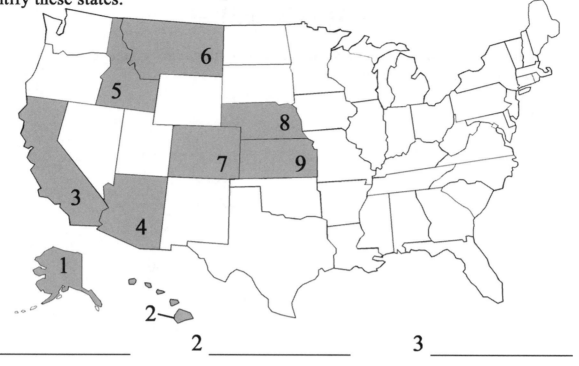

1 _____   2 _____   3 _____

4 _____   5 _____   6 _____

7 _____   8 _____   9 _____

Identify these states.

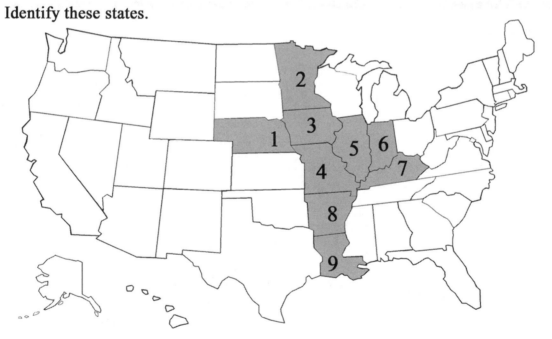

1 _____   2 _____   3 _____

4 _____   5 _____   6 _____

7 _____   8 _____   9 _____

NEVADA

CAPITAL: 1) _____

STATEHOOD: October 31, 1864

Population: 2,070,000   Area: 109,806 square miles
RANK: 35th   RANK: 7th

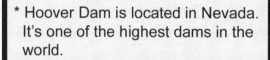

Las Vegas   Henderson   Reno

CHANGE OF CAREER.

Shortly after the Civil War began, a riverboat pilot by the name of Samuel Clemens realized that it wouldn't be profitable to work along the Mississippi River anymore. So, he packed his bags, moved to Nevada, and became a silver miner. However, he failed in the mines and settled for becoming a writer for a local newspaper, the *Daily Territorial Enterprise*. As time would prove, his career change uncovered a literary lode. Here, he practiced his writing skills and first adopted the name Mark Twain, a name that would soon be known throughout the world.

36 FACTS

* Hoover Dam is located in Nevada. It's one of the highest dams in the world.

* Nevada may be ranked 7th in land area, but 85% of it is owned by the Federal Government.

* Nevada is mostly desert, but did you know that the Sierra Nevada mountain range has areas that are covered in snow for six months of the year? It's true.

* Nevada got its name from a Spanish word that means "snow-clad."

THE SILVER STATE. Nevada is rich in silver, but the mining of gold is going strong too. So stong, in fact, that if Nevada was its own country, it would rank 2) _____ in the world; only South Africa produces more.

Note: From 1870 to 1893, gold and silver coins were minted in Carson City, Nevada. Only eight American cities have ever minted coins.

3) Find Nevada on this map and shade it in.

4) What is Nevada's abbreviation? _____

5) Approximately what percent of Nevada's land is owned by the Federal Government?

_____

6) What is the name of Nevada's largest city? _____

7) (True or False) Nevada became a state in 1854. _____

NEVADA

II. What do you remember about Nevada? Use the space below.

_____

_____

_____

III. Write the definitions to these words in the spaces provided.

Career -- _____

_____

Lode -- _____

_____

IV. Draw a picture of Nevada.

V. Connect each word to its picture.

NEVADA

NEBRASKA

MONTANA

VI. Find Nevada on this map.

VII. Unscramble these words.

LIVERS   _____

KARM WAINT   _____

HOVERO MAD   _____

ADAVEN   _____

NAME: _____

LESSON 10.2

Date: _____

NEW HAMPSHIRE
CAPITAL: 1) _____
STATEHOOD: June 21, 1788

Population: 1,281,000
RANK: 42nd

Area: 8,969 square miles
RANK: 44th

Manchester Nashua Concord

A LAND OF ALL SEASONS.
New Hampshire is known for its changeable climate. With its proximity to mountains, lakes, rivers, and the ocean, the state experiences the splendor of all four seasons. The winters are cold and long, ideal for skiing; the summers are short and cool; and falls are the perfect pictures of the glory of foliage. Each year, many come to New Hampshire to enjoy the beauty of nature.

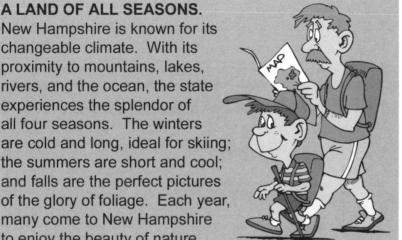

9   FACTS

* "Live Free or Die," the state motto of New Hampshire, expresses its Revolutionary War sentiments.

* Captain John 2) _____ gave New Hampshire its name. He named it in honor of Hampshire, his hometown in England.

* Mount Washington is considered to be America's windiest place. On April 12th, 1934, a wind of 234 miles per hour was measured there.

* Alan Shepard, Jr. was born in New Hampshire. He was the first American in space.

"LIVE FREE OR DIE." Of the thirteen colonies, New Hampshire was the first to declare its independence from England. Later, when the representatives of the 3) _____ colonies assembled to vote for the Declaration of Independence, the delegates from New Hampshire were given the honor of casting their votes first. That date was July 4th, 1776.

4) Find New Hampshire on this map and shade it in.

5) What is New Hampshire's abbreviation?

_____

6) According to this page, what is New Hampshire's population? _____

7) (True or False) New Hampshire was the 9th state to be admitted to the Union. _____

NEW HAMPSHIRE

II. What do you remember about New Hampsire? Use the space below.

_____

_____

_____

III. Write the definitions to these words in the spaces provided.

Colony -- _____

_____

Independence -- _____

_____

IV. Draw a picture of New Hampshire.	V. Connect each word to its picture.
	NEW HAMPSHIRE **NEVADA** **NEBRASKA**

VI. Find New Hampshire on this map.

VII. Unscramble these words.

WEN HERMASHIP _____

NOCCORD _____

JONH MITHS _____

TOVED RIFTS _____

STOP

NEW JERSEY

CAPITAL: 1) _____

STATEHOOD: December 18, 1787

Population: 8,392,000
RANK: 10th

Area: 7,418 square miles
RANK: 46th

Newark Jersey City Paterson

ELBOW ROOM? If you're looking for space, then New Jersey isn't the place. With over 1,100 people living per square mile, this East Coast state is easily the most densely populated. And because of this, it isn't too surprising to learn that 90% of New Jersians live in urban areas and that every New Jersey county is classified as a metropolitan area. What keeps the state going? Well, New Jersey is a leading industrial and chemical-producing state.

3 FACTS

* New Jersey is called the Garden State.

* President Grover Cleveland was from New Jersey. The only man to serve two nonconsecutive terms in the White House, he was the 22nd *and* 2) _____ President.

* Some other famous New Jersians include: political leader Aaron Burr, explorer Zebulon Pike, entertainer Jerry Lewis, and General Norman Schwarzkopf.

* Wow, the Statue of Liberty is NOT in New York. It's in New Jersey.

THE CROSSROADS. New Jersey played a pivotal role during the Revolutionary War. Geographically, the state was practically in the center of the nation; therefore, it was common to see both British and American troops crisscrossing the state between New York and Pennsylvania. In fact, because of its strategic location, New Jersey was the setting for more 3) _____ than any other state.

4) Find New Jersey on this map and shade it in.

5) What is New Jersey's abbreviation? _____

6) (True or False) New Jersey was the 10th state to join the Union. _____

7) What is the name of New Jersey's most populated city? _____

NEW JERSEY

II. What do you remember about New Jersey? Use the space below.

_____

_____

_____

III. Write the definitions to these words in the spaces provided.

Pivotal -- _____

_____

Revolution -- _____

_____

IV. Draw a picture of New Jersey.	V. Connect each word to its picture.
	NEW JERSEY NEW HAMPSHIRE NEVADA
VI. Find New Jersey on this map.	**VII. Unscramble these words.** STOM BASTLET _____ VOLERUTION _____ NOTRENT _____ WEN SERJEY _____

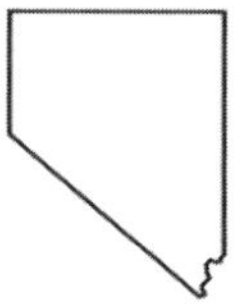

STOP

QUIZ #10

1. Three states are listed below. Color (or shade in) each of these states on the map. Then draw lines to connect each state name to its colored area.

Nevada   New Hampshire   New Jersey

2. Identify these states.

1 _____   2 _____   3 _____

4 _____   5 _____   6 _____

7 _____   8 _____   9 _____

QUIZ #10

Identify these states.

1 _____ 2 _____ 3 _____

4 _____ 5 _____ 6 _____

7 _____ 8 _____ 9 _____

Identify these states.

1 _____ 2 _____ 3 _____

4 _____ 5 _____ 6 _____

7 _____ 8 _____ 9 _____

NAME: _____

NEW MEXICO

CAPITAL: 1) _____

STATEHOOD: January 6, 1912

| Population: 2,016,000 | Area: 121,355 square miles |
| RANK: 36th | RANK: 5th |

Albuquerque   Las Cruces   Santa Fe

BEWARE, THE NIGHT.
Carlsbad Cavern is an attraction like no other. With nearly one million bats calling the sanctuary their home, the moonlit sky often becomes darkened when these creatures take to flight. One chamber in the cavern is especially huge. It's over ten football fields long and more than twenty stories high!

47 FACTS

* Did you think Denver was high? Well, at 7,000 feet above sea level, New Mexico's Santa Fe is the highest capital in America.

* BOOM! The world's first atomic bomb was detonated at the White Sands Testing Area in 1945. The development of this weapon helped to shorten the Second World 2) _____.

* Did you know that New Mexico's constitution states that it's a bilingual state? Nearly 1 in 3 citizens of New Mexico speaks 3) _____ at home.

NOT MUCH WATER. New Mexico is a very dry state, with less than 1% of its surface area being lakes and rivers. Nonetheless, the desert state has some beautiful scenery. White Sands National Monument is considered a desert, but it's not one made of sand. White gypsum crystals produce gleaming effects that attract many visitors to the wonders of New Mexico.

4) Find New Mexico on this map and shade it in.

5) What is New Mexico's abbreviation? _____

6) _____ Caverns is home to nearly one million bats.

7) (True or False) Nearly 10% of New Mexico's surface area is water. _____

NEW MEXICO

II. What do you remember about New Mexico? Use the space below.

_____

_____

_____

III. Write the definitions to these words in the spaces provided.

Gypsum --_____

_____

Sanctuary --_____

_____

IV. Draw a picture of New Mexico.	**V. Connect each word to its picture.** **NEW MEXICO** **NEW JERSEY** **NEW HAMPSHIRE**
VI. Find New Mexico on this map.	**VII. Unscramble these words.** ANTAS EF _____ COMITA MOBB _____ SERTED _____ ISHSPAN _____

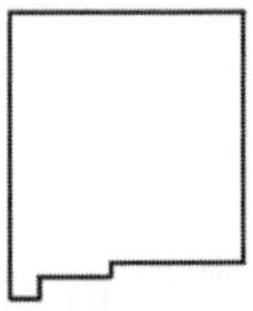

STOP

NAME: _____

Date: _____

NEW YORK

CAPITAL: 1) _____

STATEHOOD: July 26, 1788

Population: 18,250,000	Area: 47,223 square miles
RANK: 3rd	RANK: 30th

2) _____

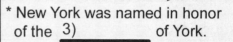
Buffalo   Rochester

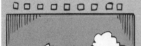

ELEVATORS AND SUBWAYS.
New York City is by far the largest city in the United States. With 8.5 million people, it more than doubles the next largest city, Los Angeles. Now, because of its huge buildings and dense population, elevators and subways have become common forms of transportation. In fact, New York City has over 700 miles of subway track to take people from one part of the city to another.

11   FACTS

* New York was named in honor of the 3) _____ of York.

* The first railroad in the United States was built in New York. It connected Schenectady to Albany.

* Did you know that New York City once served as our nation's capital?

* The headquarters for the United Nations are in New York.

* Presidents Martin Van Buren, Millard Fillmore, Theodore Roosevelt and Franklin Roosevelt were from New York.

A SAD DAY. Almost 100 years before the World Trade Center tragedies, New York City dealt with a disaster aboard the excursion ferry "The General Slocum." On June 15th, 1904, the ferry caught fire with 1,358 people on board; most of them were women and children going to a church picnic. Before lifeboats could be lowered, the wooden boat was ablaze and passengers were trapped beneath the decks. In all, 1,021 people died.

4) Find New York on this map and shade it in.

5) What is New York's abbreviation? _____

6) (True or False) New York City is the 2nd largest city in the U.S. _____

7) (Yes or No) Was New York the 3rd state to join the Union? _____

NEW YORK

II. What do you remember about New York? Use the space below.

_____

_____

_____

III. Write the definitions to these words in the spaces provided.

Excursion -- _____

_____

Duke -- _____

_____

IV. Draw a picture of New York.	**V. Connect each word to its picture.**
	NEW YORK NEW MEXICO NEW JERSEY
VI. Find New York on this map.	**VII. Unscramble these words.** KUDE FO KORY _____ DUNEIT ANTIONS _____ GIB TICY _____ ATELEVORS _____

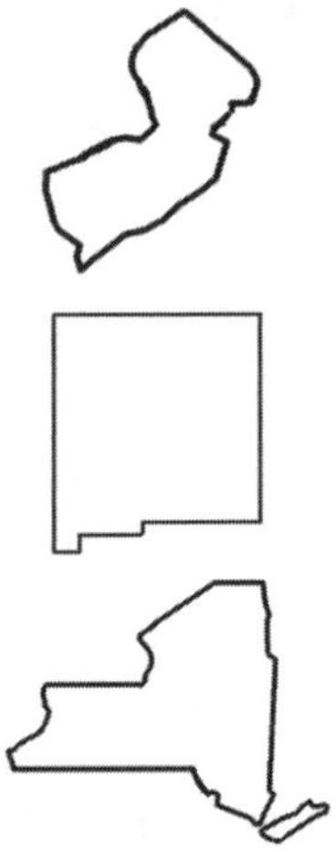

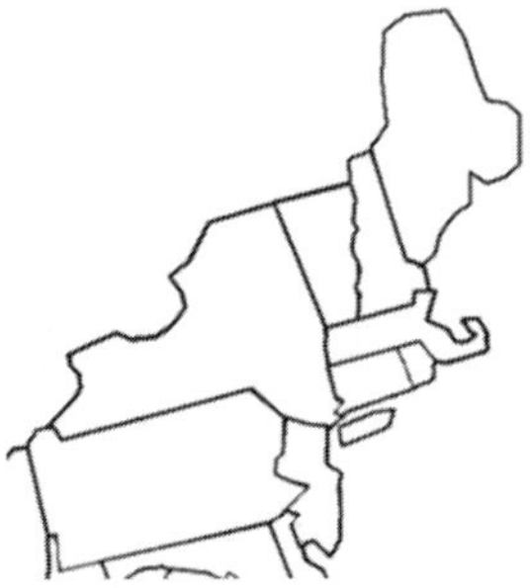

STOP

NAME: _____

NORTH CAROLINA

CAPITAL: 1) _____

STATEHOOD: November 21, 1789

Population: 8,227,000   Area: 48,718 square miles
RANK: 11th   RANK: 29th

Charlotte Raleigh Greensboro

The Wright Brothers

IT'S A BIRD... In 1903, Orville and Wilbur Wright made history by being the first men to successfully make a powered flight with an airplane. About four miles outside Kitty Hawk, the brothers took to the air on a sand mountain near the ocean. And although Kitty Hawk is often credited with being the location of this event, the actual location was at Kill Devil's Hill. Kitty Hawk was merely the place where Orville sent a telegraph containing news of their flight.

12 FACTS

* North Carolina is commonly known as the 2) _____ State.

* Presidents Andrew Johnson and James K. Polk were from North Carolina.

* Other famous North Carolinians include: First Lady Dolley Madison, Revolutionary War soldier Braxton Bragg, auto racer Richard Petty, and evangelist Billy Graham.

* On March 7th, 1914, Babe Ruth hit his first professional homerun. He was playing in Fayetteville, North Carolina at the time.

LEADING THE NATION. North Carolina is first in the nation in its production of sweet potatoes, tobacco, brick, furniture, and textiles. The state also has the distinction of being the site of England's first colony in America. Sadly, however, the colony didn't survive. In fact, all the colonists of Roanoke Island mysteriously disappeared around 1590. The only clue as to their whereabouts was the word "Croatoan." It was found etched on a log.

3) Find North Carolina on this map and shade it in.

4) What is North Carolina's abbreviation? _____

5) (True or False) James K. Polk was from North Carolina. _____

6) What is the name of North Carolina's largest city? _____

7) In what year did North Carolina become a state? _____

NORTH CAROLINA

II. What do you remember about North Carolina? Use the space below.

_____

_____

_____

III. Write the definitions to these words in the spaces provided.

Credited -- _____

_____

Professional -- _____

_____

IV. Draw a picture of North Carolina.

V. Connect each word to its picture.

NORTH CAROLINA

NEW YORK

NEW MEXICO

VI. Find North Carolina on this map.

VII. Unscramble these words.

RATHILL TATES _____

ENALPRIA _____

OARKONE _____

ASIDSAPPER _____

STOP

NAME: _____

LESSON 11.4

Date: _____

QUIZ #11

1. Three states are listed below. Color (or shade in) each of these states on the map. Then draw lines to connect each state name to its colored area.

New Mexico   North Carolina   New York

2. Identify these states.

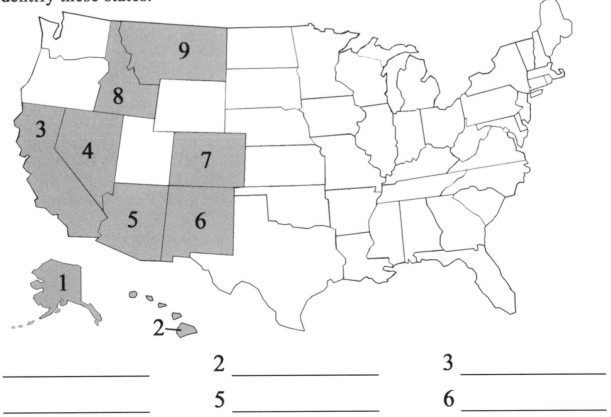

1 _____ 2 _____ 3 _____

4 _____ 5 _____ 6 _____

7 _____ 8 _____ 9 _____

QUIZ #11

Identify these states.

1 _____   2 _____   3 _____

4 _____   5 _____   6 _____

7 _____   8 _____   9 _____

Identify these states.

1 _____   2 _____   3 _____

4 _____   5 _____   6 _____

7 _____   8 _____   9 _____

NAME: _____

NORTH DAKOTA

CAPITAL: 1) _____

STATEHOOD: November 2, 1889

Population: 677,000	Area: 68,994 square miles
RANK: 48th	RANK: 17th

Fargo Bismarck Grand Forks

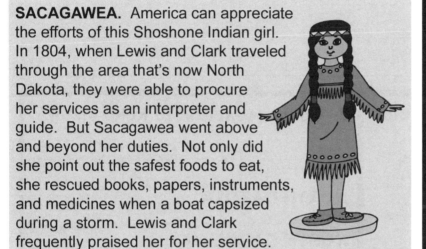

SACAGAWEA. America can appreciate the efforts of this Shoshone Indian girl. In 1804, when Lewis and Clark traveled through the area that's now North Dakota, they were able to procure her services as an interpreter and guide. But Sacagawea went above and beyond her duties. Not only did she point out the safest foods to eat, she rescued books, papers, instruments, and medicines when a boat capsized during a storm. Lewis and Clark frequently praised her for her service.

39 40 FACTS

* North Dakota is home to North America's geographic 2) _____.

* North Dakota leads the nation in its production of 3) _____.

* Did you know that North Dakota has many dinosaur fossils hidden under its soil? It's an archeological gold mine.

* North Dakota is called the Flickertail State, but what does that mean? Flickertail is another name for the Richardson ground squirrel. While running, the furry native of North Dakota sometimes flicks its tail.

WHICH STATE IS IT? Was North Dakota the 39th or 40th state to be admitted to the Union? No one really knows. On November 2nd, 1889, it and South Dakota entered the Union at exactly the same time. Therefore, when you read about either of the Dakota states, you'll find statements like "39th or 40th" attached to them.

4) Find North Dakota on this map and shade it in

5) What is North Dakota's abbreviation? _____

6) (True or False) Sacagawea was a Cherokee Indian girl.

7) (True or False) North Dakota entered the Union on the same date as South Carolina.

_____

NORTH DAKOTA

II. What do you remember about North Dakota? Use the space below.

_____

_____

_____

III. Write the definitions to these words in the spaces provided.

Interpreter -- _____

_____

Fossils -- _____

_____

IV. Draw a picture of North Dakota.	**V. Connect each word to its picture.** NORTH DAKOTA NORTH CAROLINA NEW YORK
VI. Find North Dakota on this map.	**VII. Unscramble these words.** THORN ATODAK _____ FISSOLS _____ UNDIROSA _____ WISEL & LARCK _____

OHIO

CAPITAL: 1) _____

STATEHOOD: March 1, 1803

Population: 11,428,000   Area: 40,953 square miles
RANK: 7th   RANK: 35th

Columbus Cleveland Cincinnati

ORGANIZED SPORTS. Ohioans can take pride in the fact that they helped start the growth of professional sports. In 1869, the Cincinnati Red Stockings took the field as America's first pro baseball team. That team won its first 130 games before falling to the Brooklyn Atlantics, 8-7. Also, in 1920, the first professional football league was formed in Canton, Ohio. During that year, the Akron Pros finished the season with six wins, no losses, and three ties.

17   FACTS

* Cleveland, Ohio was the first city in the world to be lighted with 2) _____.

* In 1924, Ohio's DeHart Hubbard became the first African-American to win an Olympic 3) _____ medal.

* Cleveland's Jesse Owens also won Olympic gold. In 1936, he brought home four gold medals!

* Do you live within 500 miles of Columbus, Ohio? Nearly half the people in our nation do.

* Ohio is called the Buckeye State.

ALL OR NOTHING. It's hard to believe, but seven presidents have come from the state of Ohio. They are: Ulysses S. Grant, Rutherford B. Hayes, James A. Garfield, Benjamin Harrison, William McKinley, William H. Taft, and Warren G. Harding. However, despite these lofty numbers, Ohio never produced any of the forty-five vice presidents who served our nation.

4) Find Ohio on this map and shade it in.

5) What is Ohio's abbreviation? _____

6) Ohio's largest cities are: Columbus, Cleveland, and _____.

7) (True or False) Ohio is called the Buckeye State. _____

OHIO

II. What do you remember about Ohio? Use the space below.

_____

_____

_____

III. Write the definitions to these words in the spaces provided.

Professional -- _____

_____

League -- _____

_____

IV. Draw a picture of Ohio.	V. Connect each word to its picture.
	OHIO **NORTH DAKOTA** **NORTH CAROLINA**

VI. Find Ohio on this map.	VII. Unscramble these words.
	STROPS _____ ESSEJ WENSO _____ ELCITERCITY _____ LEVELCAND _____

STOP

OKLAHOMA

CAPITAL: 1) _____

STATEHOOD: November 16, 1907

Population: 3,491,000	Area: 68,679 square miles
RANK: 28th	RANK: 19th

Oklahoma City Tulsa Norman

A REAL CHAMPION. Born in a one-room cabin in 1887, Jim Thorpe grew up to become a track, baseball, and football star. When he competed in the 1912 Olympics, he won four 2) _____ medals and the praises of Belgium's King Gustav V. "Sir," the king said, "you are the greatest athlete in the world!" To this day, there are few who would disagree.

NOTE: Jim Thorpe had a twin brother, Charlie, who died of pneumonia at the age of 8.

46 FACTS

* Choctaw was established in 1893. It's Oklahoma's 3) _____ town.

* Did you know that Boise City was the only U.S. city to be bombed during World War II? That's right. On July 5th, 1943, the U.S. military dropped some "practice" bombs on the city.

* Oklahoma City is home to the National Cowboy Hall of Fame.

* In 1935, the nation's first parking meter was installed in Oklahoma City.

THE SOONER STATE? April 22nd, 1889, was the date that the U.S. Government opened much of Oklahoma for settlement, and 50,000 people gathered to await the start of the "race" for land. However, prior to the sounding of the noonday gun, some started "sooner" than the others. Hence, the state got its nickname.

4) Find Oklahoma on this map and shade it in.

5) (Yes or No) The abbreviation for Oklahoma is OK. _____

6) What is the name of Oklahoma's 1912 Olympic champion? _____

7) (Yes or No) Oklahoma's largest city is Tulsa. _____

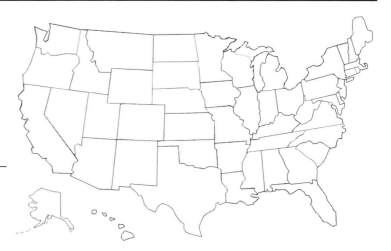

OKLAHOMA

II. What do you remember about Oklahoma? Use the space below.

_____

_____

_____

III. Write the definitions to these words in the spaces provided.

Athlete --_____

_____

Pneumonia --_____

_____

IV. Draw a picture of Oklahoma.	V. Connect each word to its picture.
	OKLAHOMA OHIO NORTH DAKOTA
VI. Find Oklahoma on this map.	**VII. Unscramble these words.** ERSOON TATES _____ MIJ PRETHO _____ YOLMPICS _____ LOOKAHAM _____

NAME: _____

Date: _____

Identify these states.

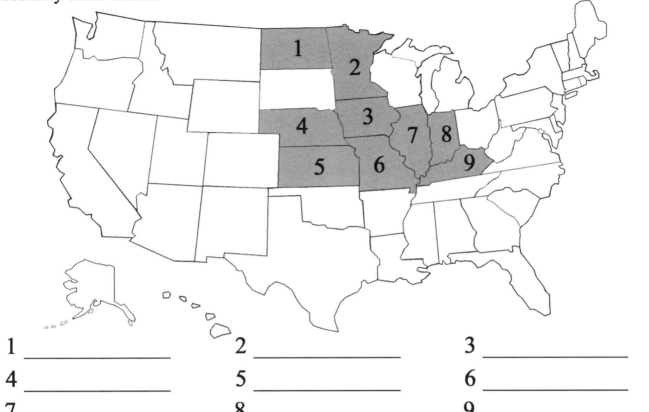

1 _____ 2 _____ 3 _____

4 _____ 5 _____ 6 _____

7 _____ 8 _____ 9 _____

Identify these states.

1 _____ 2 _____ 3 _____

4 _____ 5 _____ 6 _____

7 _____ 8 _____ 9 _____

QUIZ #12

Identify these states.

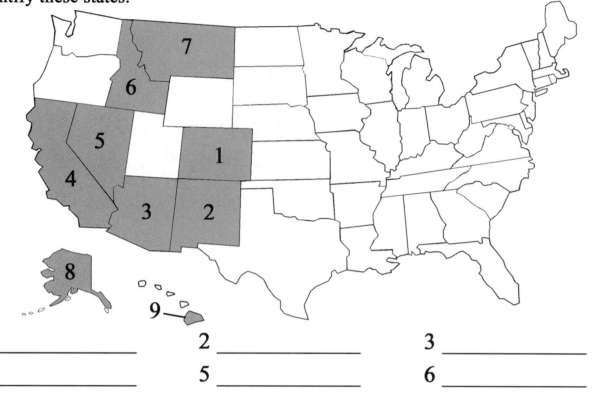

1 _____	2 _____	3 _____
4 _____	5 _____	6 _____
7 _____	8 _____	9 _____

Identify these states.

1 _____	2 _____	3 _____
4 _____	5 _____	6 _____
7 _____	8 _____	9 _____

OREGON

CAPITAL: 1) _____

STATEHOOD: February 14, 1859

Population: 3,613,000
RANK: 27th

Area: 96,003 square miles
RANK: 10th

Portland   Salem   Eugene

BOO! No, Oregon doesn't have the most ghosts, but it does claim to have the most ghost towns! Many towns, like Yellow Dog and Raw Dog, were doomed to perish when newly-built roads made stagecoach stops unnecessary. Others faded when gold could no longer be found, and then there's the story of Antelope. First hit by a fire, the rebuilt town faded into history when a railroad station was built in a nearby town.

33 FACTS

* The deepest lake in America is Oregon's Crater Lake. It's the remains of an ancient 2) _____ .

* Oregon is also home to America's deepest canyon. It's over 8,000 feet deep!

* Oregon has a nickname. It's called the 3) _____ State.

* The word *Oregon* means...? Well, no one really knows the answer to that question. It's unknown.

* Wow! Oregon doesn't have any SELF-service gas stations.

OREGON. During the late 1700s and early 1800s, hunters and trappers pushed westward to Oregon. Here, they found the land teeming with beaver. Companies established themselves, and pioneers soon followed to tame the fertile soil. Afterwards, gold was discovered and even more settlers moved to the area. However, many of them turned to the logging and fishing industries when their search for gold didn't "pan out."

4) Find Oregon on this map and shade it in.

5) On what date did Oregon become a state?
_____

6) (True or False) Oregon's abbreviation is ON. _____

7) According to this page, what is Oregon's population? _____

OREGON

II. What do you remember about Oregon? Use the space below.

_____

_____

_____

III. Write the definitions to these words in the spaces provided.

Ancient --_____

_____

Teeming --_____

_____

IV. Draw a picture of Oregon.

V. Connect each word to its picture.

OREGON

OKLAHOMA

OHIO

VI. Find Oregon on this map.

VII. Unscramble these words.

VERBEA TATES   _____

STRAPPER   _____

GOLGING   _____

STOGH STOWN   _____

STOP

PENNSYLVANIA

CAPITAL: 1) _____

STATEHOOD: December 12, 1787

Population: 12,281,000   Area: 44,820 square miles
RANK: 5th   RANK: 32nd

Philadelphia   Pittsburgh   Allentown

A LEADER. The city of Philadelphia has been instrumental to the growth of our country. In 1776, representatives from the colonies met there, debated, and eventually signed the Declaration of Independence. In 1784, it became the home of our nation's first newspaper. For a time, it served as our nation's capital, and it has the distinction of becoming the first American city to have a zoo. Today, Philadelphia has many historical landmarks that can be visited by those who love history.

2 FACTS

* The *WORDS TO REMEMBER* (shown in purple) come from the 2) _____ of Independence.

* The nation's first public zoo was founded by Benjamin Franklin in Philadelphia.

* Pennsylvania is named after its founder, William Penn. Many of the democratic principles that he set forth served as an inspiration for the U.S. 3) _____ .

* Famous Pennsylvanians include: President James Buchanan, explorer Daniel Boone, and Civil War General George McClellan.

WORDS TO REMEMBER. "When in the Course of human Events, it becomes necessary for one People to dissolve the political bands which have connected them with one another, and to assume, among the Powers of the Earth, the separate and equal Station to which the Laws of Nature and of Nature's God entitle them, a decent Respect to the Opinions of Mankind requires that they should declare the Causes which impel them to the Separation."

4) Find Pennsylvania on this map and shade it in.

5) What is Pennsylvania's abbreviation? _____

6) What is the name of Pennsylvania's largest city? _____

6) Who founded our nation's first public zoo?

_____

PENNSYLVANIA

II. What do you remember about Pennsylvania? Use the space below.

_____

_____

_____

III. Write the definitions to these words in the spaces provided.

Instrumental -- _____

_____

Liberty -- _____

_____

IV. Draw a picture of Pennsylvania.	**V. Connect each word to its picture.** **PENNSYLVANIA** **OREGON** **OKLAHOMA**
VI. Find Pennsylvania on this map.	**VII. Unscramble these words.** CLARATIONED _____ DECEPENDENIN _____ ADPHILELPHIA _____ AVANPENNSILY _____

RHODE ISLAND

CAPITAL: 1) _____

STATEHOOD: May 29, 1790

Population: 1,012,000   Area: 1,045 square miles
RANK: 43rd   RANK: 50th

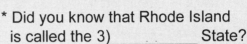
Providence Warwick Cranston

MEASURING UP. You bet, when it comes to land size, Rhode Island is the smallest state in the nation. With only 1,045 square miles of land, it would still have to double in size to move up to the 49th spot. But, as history has shown, Rhode Island has been instrumental in American history. In fact, Thomas Jefferson and John 2) _____ acknowledged that Roger Williams, the founder of Rhode Island, was the originator of America's freedom of religion, speech, and public assembly.

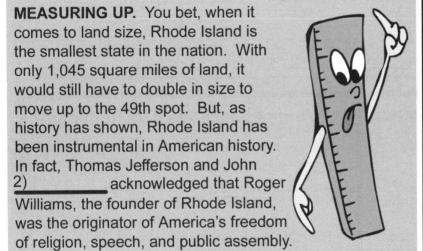

13   FACTS

* Did you know that Rhode Island is called the 3) _____ State?

* The first British soldiers to fight in the American Revolution landed in Newport.

* America's first African-American regiment fought against the British in Rhode Island.

* America's oldest schoolhouse was built in Portsmouth in 1716.

* Samuel Slater's Rhode Island cotton mill is credited with starting our nation's Industrial Revolution.

A PRELUDE TO WAR. On June 10th, 1772, four years prior to the Revolutionary War, Rhode Islanders were the first to take military action against the English. What did they do? They sunk one of the King's merchant ships, "The Gaspee." A few weeks later, a London newspaper described the incident as the doings of a bunch of smugglers who burned the boat and "carried their commerce in triumph to their own habitations."

4) Find Rhode Island on this map and shade it in.

5) What is the abbreviation for Rhode Island?

_____

6) In the U.S., Alaska is ranked 1st in land size. What is Rhode Island's rank? _____

7) (True or False) "The Gaspee" was destroyed on June 10th, 1776. _____

RHODE ISLAND

II. What do you remember about Rhode Island? Use the space below.

_____

_____

_____

III. Write the definitions to these words in the spaces provided.

Regiment -- _____

_____

Habitation -- _____

_____

IV. Draw a picture of Rhode Island.	**V. Connect each word to its picture.** **RHODE ISLAND** **PENNSYLVANIA** **OREGON**
VI. Find Rhode Island on this map.	**VII. Unscramble these words.** NOCEA TATES _____ MALLESTS _____ VIDPROENCE _____ HODER LANDIS _____

NAME: _____ QUIZ #13 LESSON 13.4

Date: _____

Identify these states.

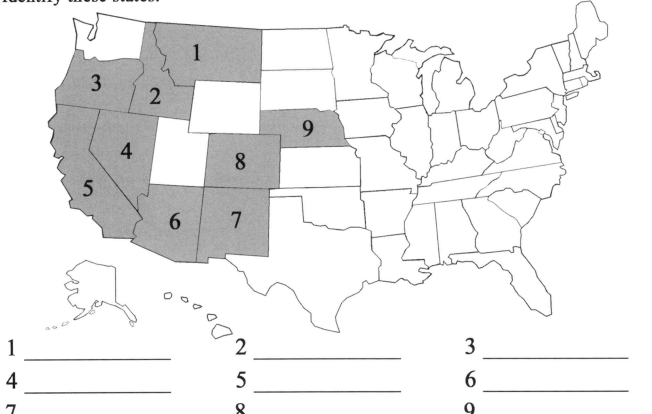

1 _____ 2 _____ 3 _____

4 _____ 5 _____ 6 _____

7 _____ 8 _____ 9 _____

Identify these states.

1 _____ 2 _____ 3 _____

4 _____ 5 _____ 6 _____

7 _____ 8 _____ 9 _____

QUIZ #13

Identify these states.

1 _____   2 _____   3 _____

4 _____   5 _____   6 _____

7 _____   8 _____   9 _____

Identify these states.

1 _____   2 _____   3 _____

4 _____   5 _____   6 _____

7 _____   8 _____   9 _____

SOUTH CAROLINA

CAPITAL: 1) _____

STATEHOOD: May 23, 1788

Population: 4,033,000	Area: 30,111 square miles
RANK: 26th	RANK: 40th

Columbia
Charleston
North Charleston

CELEBRATIONS. Many don't know it, but Georgia isn't the leading producer of peaches; South Carolina is. Every July, the city of Gaffney hosts a ten-day festival to celebrate the tasty fruit. But the state also has festivals for other delicacies. Ware Shoals has a Catfish Festival; Beaufort hosts a Shrimp Festival; and Little River has a Blue Crab Festival. Then there's the celebration hosted by Myrtle Beach. Every year, it has the Sun Fun Festival.

8 FACTS

* South Carolina is called the Palmetto State. When the British tried to capture a fort made of Palmetto logs, their cannonballs simply bounced off the spongy wood.

* Does South Carolina have its own Loch Ness monster? Some think that a creature resembling a snake and something prehistoric lives in Lake Murray.

* Famous South Carolinians include: President Andrew Jackson, General Francis Marion, and civil rights leader 2) _____ Jackson.

THE CIVIL WAR. On April 10th, 1861, General Beauregard of the provisional Confederate forces at Charleston demanded the surrender of the 3) _____ garrison at Fort Sumter, which was in Charleston Harbor. Union Major Robert Anderson refused to comply and the Confederate batteries opened fire. The Civil War had begun. And although no one died in this first exchange, future battles wouldn't be so bloodless. Over 600,000 would die in the years to come.

4) Find South Carolina on this map and fill it in.

5) What is South Carolina's abbreviation? _____

6) (True or False) South Carolina was the 12th state to enter the Union. _____

7) What is the name of South Carolina's largest city? _____

SOUTH CAROLINA

II. What do you remember about South Carolina? Use the space below.

_____

_____

_____

III. Write the definitions to these words in the spaces provided.

Provisional -- _____

_____

Festivals -- _____

_____

IV. Draw a picture of South Carolina.

V. Connect each word to its picture.

SOUTH CAROLINA

RHODE ISLAND

PENNSYLVANIA

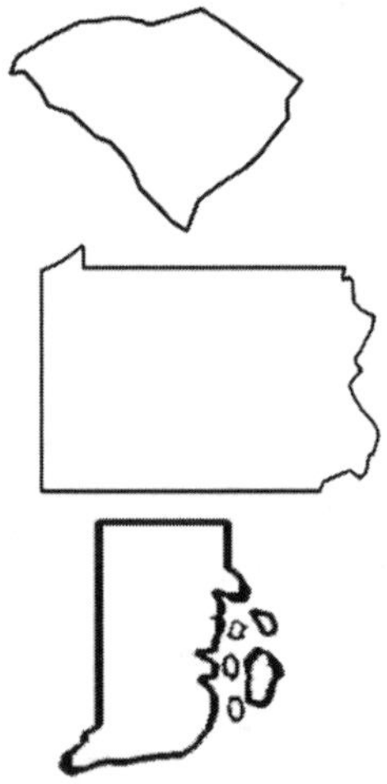

VI. Find South Carolina on this map.

VII. Unscramble these words.

LIVIC ARW   _____

FROT MUSTER   _____

ONIUN   _____

CODFENERACY _____

STOP

SOUTH DAKOTA

CAPITAL: 1) _____

STATEHOOD: November 2, 1889

Population: 810,000	Area: 75,884 square miles
RANK: 45th	RANK: 16th

Sioux Falls Rapid City Aberdeen

39 40 FACTS

* South Dakota is home to the world's largest petrified wood park. This area also contains many 2) _____ fossils.

* South Dakota is called the Coyote State.

* If you thought Mount Rushmore was big, then just wait until the Crazy Horse mountain project is finished. This sculpture will be 563 feet tall!

* Wind Cave is huge. With nearly 82 miles of passageways, it's quite a tourist attraction.

FAMOUS FACES. Although less than one million people live there, a variety of recognizable names have come from South Dakota: Vice President Hubert Humphrey, TV newscaster Tom Brokaw, baseball manager Sparky Anderson, politician George McGovern, and actress Cheryl Ladd, to name a few.

A BEAUTIFUL CARVING. South Dakota is home to one of America's greatest monuments, Mount Rushmore. The sculpture of George Washington, Thomas Jefferson, Theodore Roosevelt, and Abraham Lincoln draws many tourists each year. The project in honor of these four presidents began in 1927, cost one million dollars, and took sculptor Gutzon Borglum nearly fourteen 3) _____ to complete.

4) Find South Dakota on this map and shade it in.

5) What is South Dakota's abbreviation? _____

6) (True or False) South Dakota is called the Prairie Dog State. _____

7) (True or False) Mount Rushmore is located in South Dakota. _____

SOUTH DAKOTA

II. What do you remember about South Dakota? Use the space below.

_____

_____

_____

III. Write the definitions to these words in the spaces provided.

Sculpture -- _____

_____

Tourist -- _____

_____

IV. Draw a picture of South Dakota.	**V. Connect each word to its picture.**
	**SOUTH DAKOTA** **SOUTH CAROLINA** **RHODE ISLAND**
VI. Find South Dakota on this map.	**VII. Unscramble these words.**
	STOURITS _____ REPIDSENTS _____ RERUSHMO _____ OUTHS ODAKTA _____

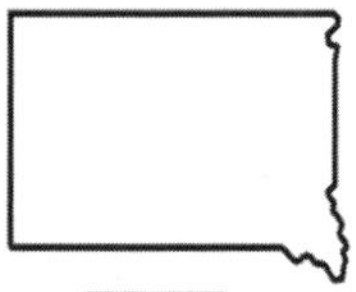

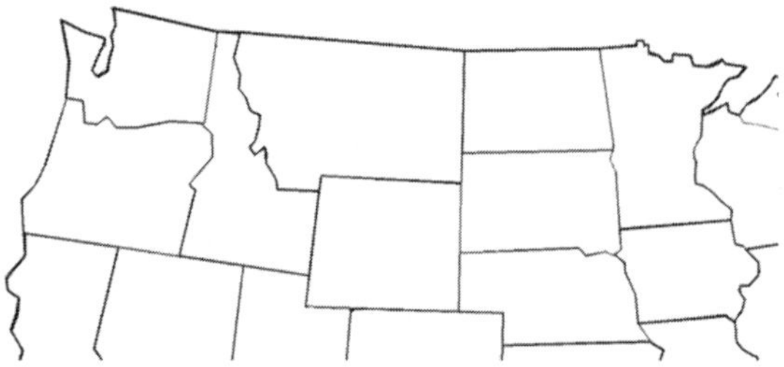

STOP

TENNESSEE

CAPITAL: 1) _____

STATEHOOD: June 1, 1796

Population: 5,966,000   Area: 41,220 square miles
RANK: 16th   RANK: 34th

Memphis Nashville Knoxville

THE VOLUNTEER STATE. During the War of 1812, many Tennesseans volunteered to fight against the British. One battle where they served with extreme valor was the Battle of New 2) _____. Tennessean Andrew Jackson, who would later become president of the United States, successfully set up defensive positions against the British at this battle. His victory was one key reason for his election and the state's right to be proudly called the Volunteer State.

16 FACTS

* Following the assassination of Abraham Lincoln, Tennessean Andrew Johnson (not Jackson) became 3) _____.

* The first female U.S. senator was from Tennessee. Her name was Hattie Caraway.

* Jackson was the home of Casey Jones, the famous railroad engineer who died when his train crashed in 1900.

* The Great Smoky Mountains National Park is the most visited national park in America.

COUNTRY MUSIC CAPITAL OF THE WORLD. Nashville, Tennessee is home to The Grand Ole Opry, a centerpiece for country music singers. Since 1925, the musical theater has been broadcasting on the radio every Friday and Saturday night (a record for the airwaves). Some of the names that have made the Opry famous are: Uncle Dave Macon, Minnie Pearl, Eddy Arnold, and Pee Wee King.

4) Find Tennessee on this map and shade it in.

5) (True or False) Tennessee's abbreviation is TN. _____

6) In what city will you find the Grand Ole Opry?

_____

7) In what year did Tennessee become a state?

_____

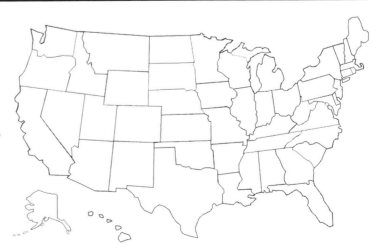

TENNESSEE

II. What do you remember about Tennessee? Use the space below.

_____

_____

_____

III. Write the definitions to these words in the spaces provided.

Volunteer -- _____

_____

Valor -- _____

_____

IV. Draw a picture of Tennessee.	**V. Connect each word to its picture.** TENNESSEE SOUTH DAKOTA SOUTH CAROLINA
VI. Find Tennessee on this map.	**VII. Unscramble these words.** REVOLUNTE _____ RAW FO 1281 _____ LORAV _____ SENTENEES _____

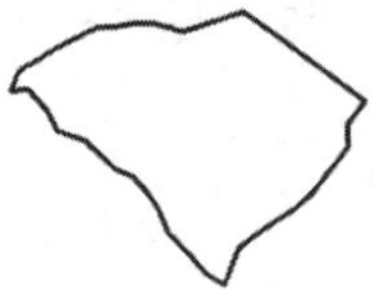

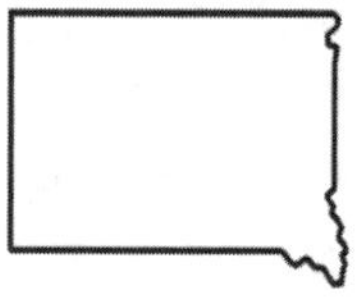

STOP

Identify these states.

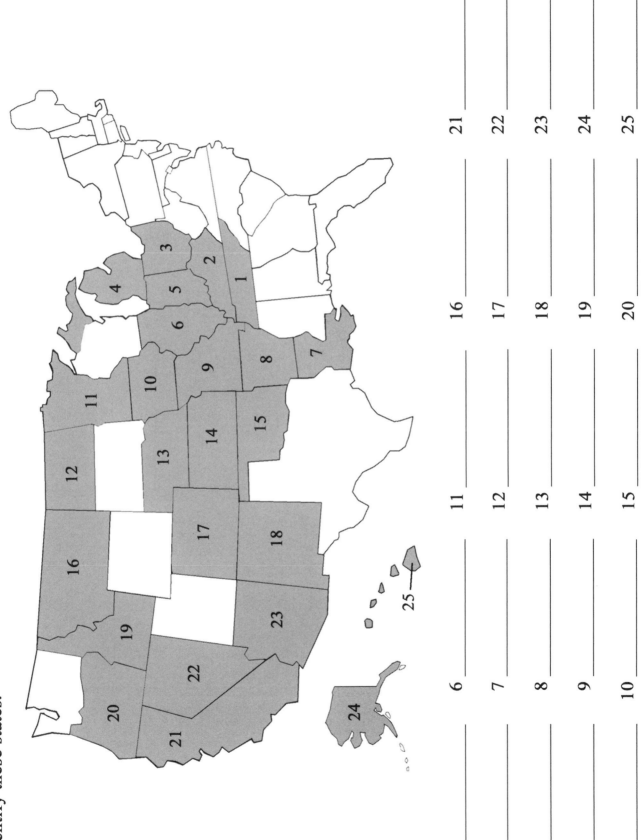

1 _____

2 _____

3 _____

4 _____

5 _____

6 _____

7 _____

8 _____

9 _____

10 _____

11 _____

12 _____

13 _____

14 _____

15 _____

16 _____

17 _____

18 _____

19 _____

20 _____

21 _____

22 _____

23 _____

24 _____

25 _____

Identify these states.

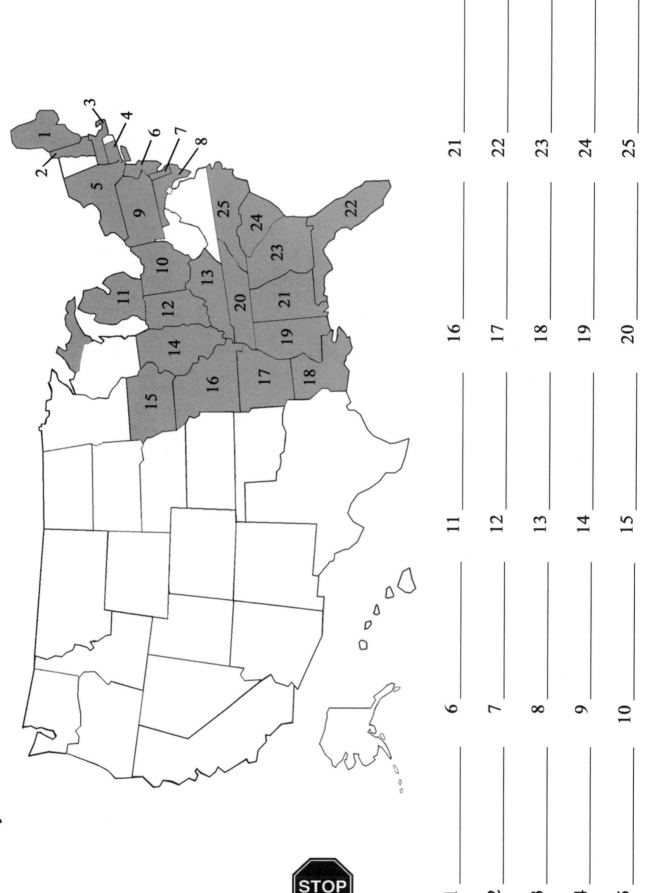

1 _____

2 _____

3 _____

4 _____

5 _____

6 _____

7 _____

8 _____

9 _____

10 _____

11 _____

12 _____

13 _____

14 _____

15 _____

16 _____

17 _____

18 _____

19 _____

20 _____

21 _____

22 _____

23 _____

24 _____

25 _____

STOP

NAME: _____

TEXAS

CAPITAL: 1) _____

STATEHOOD: December 29, 1845

LESSON 15.1

Date: _____

Population: 21,487,000	Area: 261,914 square miles
RANK: 2nd	RANK: 2nd

Houston San Antonio Dallas

THE LONE STAR. In the early 1800s, Texas was part of Mexico and many Americans had settled there. Fearing that the influx of foreigners would lead to rebellion, Mexico forbade further immigration of Americans into Texas. This policy infuriated American-born Texans, led to a few skirmishes, and sent the land into war by 1835. With the help of Sam Bowie, Davy Crockett, Sam Houston, William Travis, and Stephen Austin, Texas won its independence and became its own country. That's right, its own *country*! But this didn't last long. In 1845, Texas joined the United States by becoming the 28th state.

28 FACTS

* Texas is called the Lone Star State.

* Presidents Lyndon B. Johnson and Dwight D. Eisenhower were born in Texas.

* President George Bush and his son, President George W. Bush, are residents of Texas.

* Texas' King Ranch is big, big, big! In fact, it's bigger than the whole state of 2) _____ Island!

* In 1900, over 8,000 died when a hurricane struck Galveston. It was our nation's worst natural disaster.

BLACK GOLD! Texas has oil and lots of it. In 2004, the state produced over one million barrels a day, making it the number one producing state. As a whole, the nation pumped out 5.4 million barrels a day. Therefore, with Texas bringing in nearly 20% of the nation's crude, we can be thankful that it's no longer its own country!

3) Find Texas on this map and shade it in.

4) What is the abbreviation for Texas? _____

5) In what year did Texas become a state?

   _____

6) What country did Texans fight to gain their independence? _____

7) (True or False) In 2000, over 8,000 died when a hurricane struck Galveston. _____

TEXAS

II. What do you remember about Texas? Use the space below.

_____

_____

_____

III. Write the definitions to these words in the spaces provided.

Skirmishes --

_____

_____

Rebellion --

_____

_____

IV. Draw a picture of Texas.	**V. Connect each word to its picture.**
	TEXAS TENNESSEE SOUTH DAKOTA
VI. Find Texas on this map.	**VII. Unscramble these words.**
	TAXES _____ EXMICO _____ VOLUTIONER _____ WEN UCONTRY _____

NAME: _____

LESSON 15.2

Date: _____

UTAH

CAPITAL: 1) _____

STATEHOOD: January 4, 1896

Population: 2,411,000   Area: 82,168 square miles
RANK: 34th   RANK: 12th

45 FACTS

* Brigham Young led the first group of non-native Americans to the land that is now Utah.

* Utah is called the Beehive State, but not because of its insect population. No, the symbol merely represents the diligence and thrift of Utah's citizens.

* A+. Utah has the highest literacy rate in America.

* In 2002, the XIX Winter Olympic Games were held in Utah, where yearly snowfall can surpass 500 inches in the mountains.

Salt Lake City   West Valley City   Provo

THE MEETING POINT. Prior to the invention of the car and the making of highways, the necessity of creating a railroad to bridge the gap between America's east and west coast was a priority. On May 10th, 1869, this project was completed in what is now Utah. Silver and gold spikes were driven into the last rail to honor this great event.

A UNIQUE PLACE. Utah's Great Salt Lake is very special. Although it covers more than 2,100 square miles, the huge lake only has an average depth of 13 feet! But, if anything sets this lake apart from others, it's the saltiness of the water. With a salinity of nearly 12%, the Great Salt Lake is MUCH saltier than the ocean. In fact, it's so 2) _____ that people can easily stay afloat.

3) Find Utah on this map and shade it in.

4) What is Utah's abbreviation? _____

5) In what year did Utah become a state?

_____

6) Utah is called the _____ State.

7) According to this page, what is the population of Utah? _____

UTAH

II. What do you remember about Utah? Use the space below.

_____

_____

_____

III. Write the definitions to these words in the spaces provided.

Thrift -- _____

_____

Diligence -- _____

_____

IV. Draw a picture of Utah.	**V. Connect each word to its picture.**
	UTAH TEXAS TENNESSEE
VI. Find Utah on this map.	**VII. Unscramble these words.**
	LATS KALE _____ HEBEIVE TATES _____ DRAILORA _____ HUTA _____

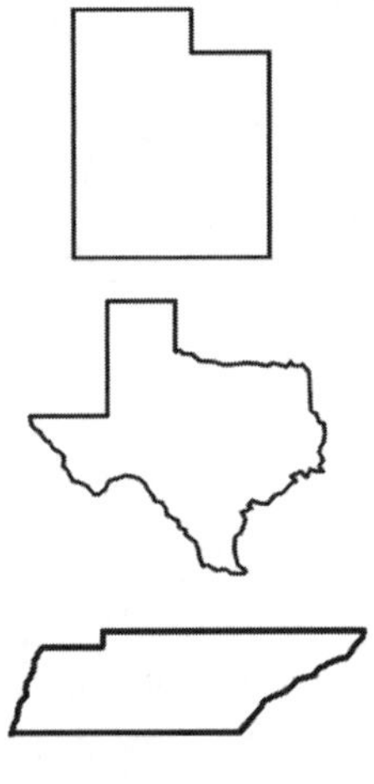

STOP

VERMONT

CAPITAL: 1) _____

STATEHOOD: March 4, 1791

Population: 638,000
RANK: 49th

Area: 9,249 square miles
RANK: 43rd

Burlington   Rutland   South Burlington

RICH IN BEAUTY. Vermont is called the Green Mountain State for good reason. It has over 220 mountains that exceed 2,000 feet in elevation! Snow skiing is very popular in the state, as vacationers from around the country come in droves to enjoy the slopes that await. But tourism isn't Vermont's only means of surviving: the state is the nation's leading producer of maple syrup; it supplies half the milk that New Englanders consume; and it produces large amounts of apples, potatoes, honey, and lumber.

14 FACTS

* Vermont's state motto is:
" 2) _____ and Unity."

* Famous Vermonters include: President Chester Arthur, President Calvin Coolidge, Admiral George Dewey, and religious leader Brigham Young.

* With under 10,000 people, Montpelier is America's least populated state 3) _____ .

* Before becoming a state, Vermont was claimed by both New York and New Hampshire.

INDEPENDENT. When speaking of Vermont, the Georgia state legislature once said that "the whole state should be made into an island and towed out to sea." Although the words were meant as an insult, the nation can take pride in many of the ideals that this state holds. For instance, Vermont demonstrated the true meaning of freedom by being the *first* state to outlaw slavery.

Free!

4) Find Vermont on this map and shade it in.

5) (True or False) Vermont's abbreviation is VM. _____

6) California is ranked 1st in population. What is Vermont's rank? _____

7) (True or False) Vermont was the 14th state to be admitted to the Union. _____

VERMONT

II. What do you remember about Vermont? Use the space below.

_____

_____

_____

III. Write the definitions to these words in the spaces provided.

Syrup -- _____

_____

Tourism -- _____

_____

IV. Draw a picture of Vermont.	V. Connect each word to its picture.
	VERMONT UTAH TEXAS

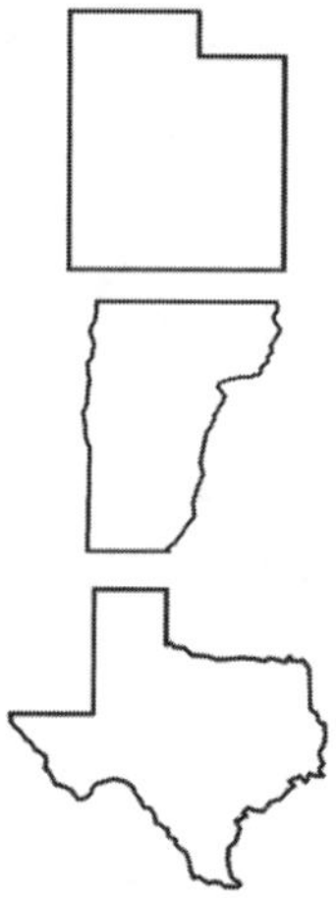

VI. Find Vermont on this map.

VII. Unscramble these words.

MOUNSTAIN   _____

NOWS ISKING   _____

ROUTISM   _____

MONTREV   _____

STOP

AME: _____

QUIZ #15

LESSON 15.4

Date: _____

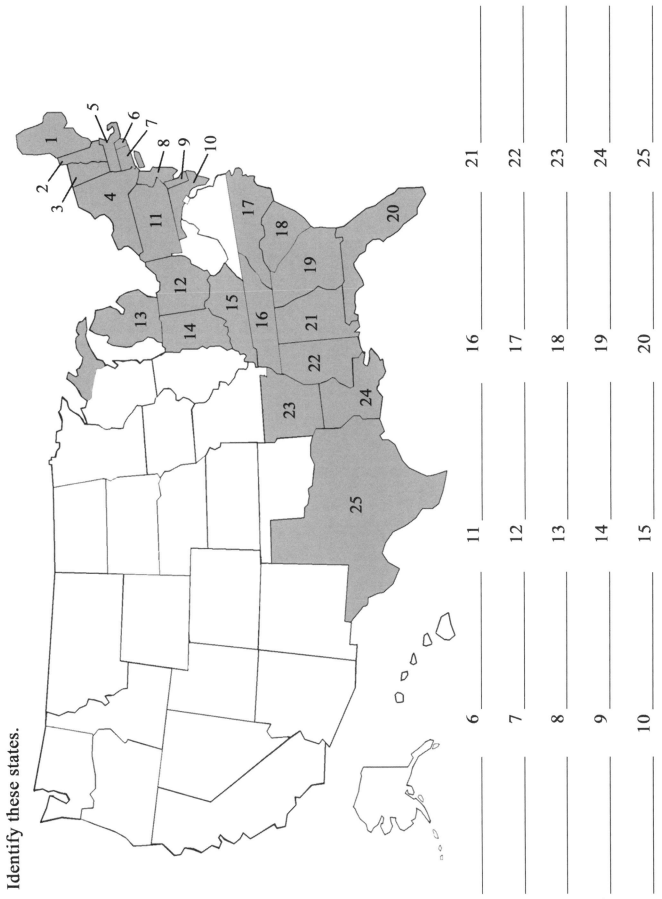

Identify these states.

1 _____
2 _____
3 _____
4 _____
5 _____

6 _____
7 _____
8 _____
9 _____
10 _____

11 _____
12 _____
13 _____
14 _____
15 _____

16 _____
17 _____
18 _____
19 _____
20 _____

21 _____
22 _____
23 _____
24 _____
25 _____

QUIZ #15

LESSON 15.4

Date: _____

Identify these states.

1 _____

2 _____

3 _____

4 _____

5 _____

6 _____

7 _____

8 _____

9 _____

10 _____

11 _____

12 _____

13 _____

14 _____

15 _____

16 _____

17 _____

18 _____

19 _____

20 _____

21 _____

22 _____

23 _____

24 _____

25 _____

STOP

VIRGINIA

CAPITAL: 1) _____

STATEHOOD: June 25, 1788

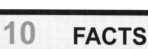

Population: 7,324,000	Area: 39,598 square miles
RANK: 12th	RANK: 37th

Virginia Beach Norfolk Chesapeake

BATTLE-TESTED. Virginia has been the field of many battles. In 1781, during the Revolutionary War, Yorktown was the site of Lord Cornwallis' defeat to George Washington. Then, years later, Confederate General Robert E. Lee was defeated by the Union army during the Civil War. With each of these surrenders, our nation was able to witness the end of two major wars.

10 FACTS

* Virginia was named in honor of England's Queen Elizabeth I.

* Famous Virginians include: Henry Clay, Robert E. Lee, Sam Houston, Booker T. Washington, Patrick 2) _____ and Nat Turner.

* In addition to being called the Old Dominion State, Virginia is called the Mother of States. Why? Well, West Virginia, Ohio, Kentucky, Indiana, Illinois, Wisconsin, and parts of Minnesota were all once part of Virginia.

* Tobacco is Virginia's major cash crop.

EIGHT IS ENOUGH? 3) _____ is often referred to as the Mother of Presidents because eight Virginians have held the highest post in the land. They are: George Washington, Thomas Jefferson, James Madison, James Monroe, William Henry Harrison, John Tyler, Zachary Taylor, and Woodrow Wilson. The only other state that's close to Virginia's record is Ohio with seven presidents.

4) Find Virginia on this map and shade it in.

5) What is Virginia's abbreviation? _____

6) (True or False) The Battle of Yorktown was fought in 1781. _____

7) Who was Virginia named in honor of?

_____

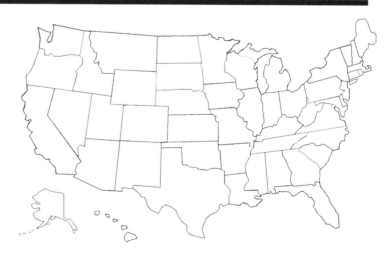

VIRGINIA

II. What do you remember about Virginia? Use the space below.

_____

_____

_____

III. Write the definitions to these words in the spaces provided.

Dominion -- _____

_____

Surrender -- _____

_____

IV. Draw a picture of Virginia.

V. Connect each word to its picture.

VIRGINIA

VERMONT

UTAH

VI. Find Virginia on this map.

VII. Unscramble these words.

IDENTPRESS _____

NASHINGTOW _____

JOFFERSEN _____

ONMADIS _____

WASHINGTON

CAPITAL: 1) _____

STATEHOOD: November 11, 1889

| Population: 6,258,000 | Area: 66,582 square miles |
| RANK: 14th | RANK: 20th |

Seattle Spokane Tacoma

OUTDOOR FUN. If you like outdoor adventure, Washington is the place to be. Whitewater rafting is a year-round sport, with spring runoff of mountain snow and steady amounts of rain continually feeding the state's many rivers. But, if that isn't your idea of fun, you could always try one of the state's other popular activities: hiking, camping, mountainbiking, fishing, skiing, snowboarding, horseback riding, or kayaking. No doubt, Washington has it all!

42 FACTS

* As its state flag suggests, Washington was named in honor of our nation's 2) _____ president.

* Washington's highest point is Mount Rainier. It was named after Peter Rainier, a British soldier.

* Medina is the home of Bill Gates, the wealthiest man in the world.

* Washington's King County was originally named after Vice President William King. However, in 1986, it was renamed in honor of civil rights leader Dr. Martin Luther 3) _____ .

A SLEEPING GIANT. Lewis and Clark described Mount Saint Helens as "perhaps the greatest pinnacle in America," but many local Indians avoided the sleeping volcano, calling it by a name meaning "fire mountain." On May 18th, 1990, the "fire mountain" came to life. After the mountain's north side gave way, a 500-degree cloud of smoke and ash killed everything within 10 miles of the north side.

4) Find Washington on this map and shade it in.

5) (True or False) Washington's abbreviation is WA. _____

6) What is the name of Washington's largest city? _____

7) Lewis and Clark described Mount Saint _____ as "perhaps the greatest pinnacle in America."

WASHINGTON

II. What do you remember about Washington? Use the space below.

_____

_____

_____

III. Write the definitions to these words in the spaces provided.

Volcano -- _____

_____

Eruption -- _____

_____

IV. Draw a picture of Washington.	**V. Connect each word to its picture.**
	WASHINGTON **VIRGINIA** **VERMONT**
VI. Find Washington on this map.	**VII. Unscramble these words.** VALCONO _____ AINTS SHELEN _____ ONERUPTI _____ SHAWINGTON _____

STOP

NAME: _____

Date: _____

WEST VIRGINIA

CAPITAL: 1) _____

STATEHOOD: June 20, 1863

Population: 1,849,000   Area: 24,087 square miles
RANK: 37th   RANK: 41st

Charleston Huntington Parkersburg

COAL. The economy of West Virginia and the nation depends heavily upon the ability to mine coal that hides beneath the soil. With that in mind, West Virginia is a leader in this endeavor, accounting for nearly 15% of the nation's coal and 50% of U.S. coal exports.

NOTE: More than half our nation's electricity is generated from 2) _____ .

35 FACTS

* In 1870, the first brick street in the world was laid in Charleston.

* West Virginian Chester Merriman was the youngest American to serve during World War I. He was only fourteen years old when he enlisted.

* The Golden Delicious Apple had its beginning in Clay County, 3) _____ Virginia.

* On July 1st, 1921, West Virginia became the first state to institute a sales tax.

THE GREAT SPLIT. West Virginia became a state during the Civil War after it broke away from the Confederate state of Virginia. By proclamation, President Lincoln paved the way for the citizens of Virginia's western area (who mostly sympathized with the North) to gain their sovereignty and become part of the Union. Because of this, West Virginia is sometimes called the northernmost southern state and the southernmost northern state.

4) Find West Virginia on this map and shade it in.

5) What is West Virginia's abbreviation? _____

6) Prior to the Civil War, West Virginia was part of what other state? _____

7) Chester _____ was the youngest American to serve during World War I.

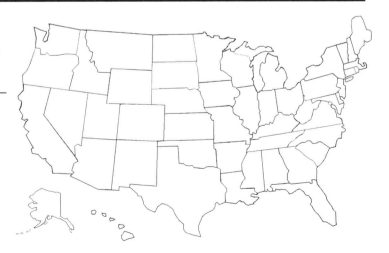

WEST VIRGINIA

LESSON 16.3

II. What do you remember about West Virginia? Use the space below.

_____

_____

_____

III. Write the definitions to these words in the spaces provided.

Proclamation -- _____

_____

Sovereignty -- _____

_____

IV. Draw a picture of West Virginia.

V. Connect each word to its picture.

WEST VIRGINIA

WASHINGTON

VIRGINIA

VI. Find West Virginia on this map.

VII. Unscramble these words.

VILIC AWR _____

BOKER AYAW _____

WEN TASET _____

STEW GVIRINIA _____

STOP

NAME: ____________________ QUIZ #16 LESSON 16.4

Date: __________

Identify these states.

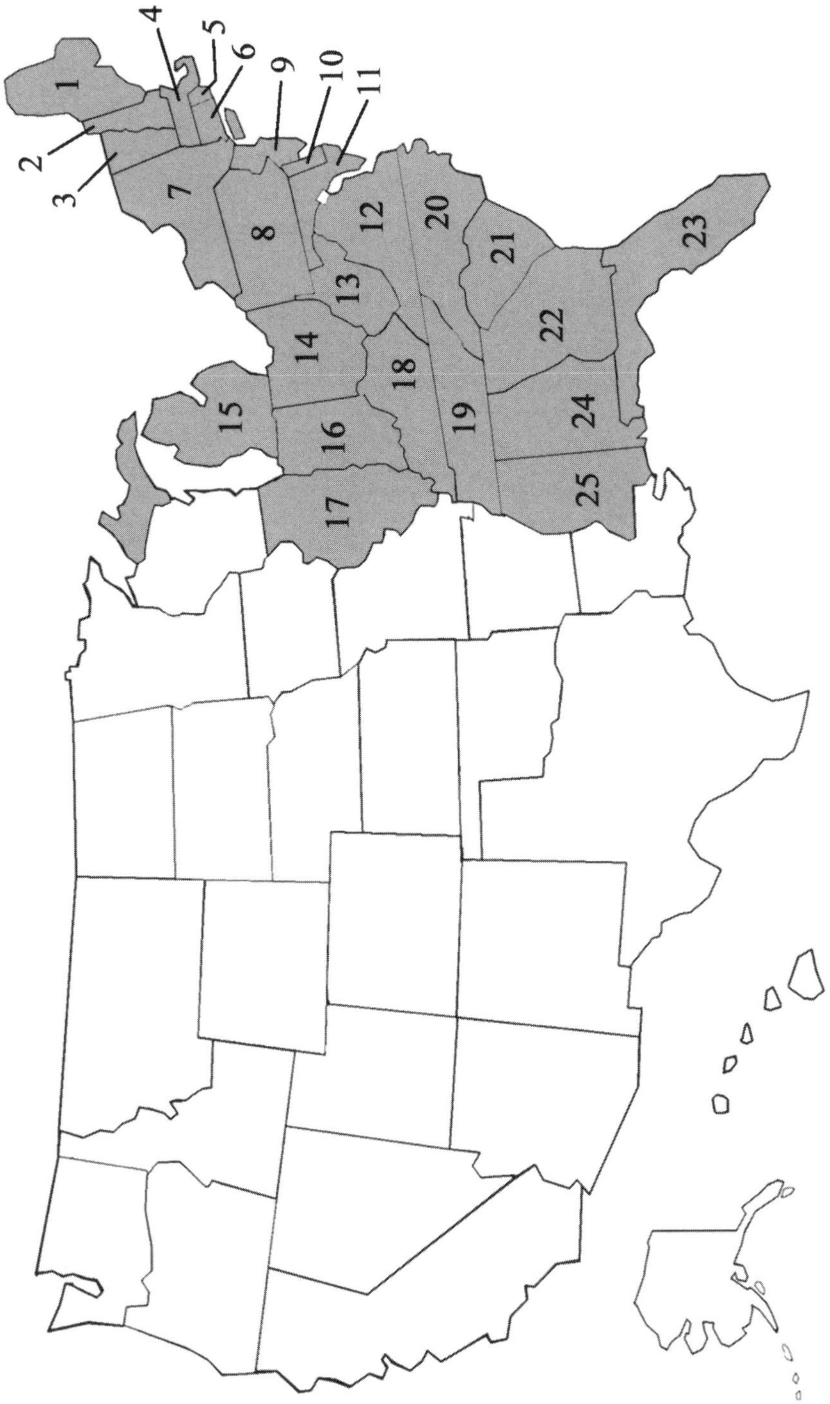

1 ____________ 2 ____________ 3 ____________ 4 ____________ 5 ____________

6 ____________ 7 ____________ 8 ____________ 9 ____________ 10 ____________

11 ____________ 12 ____________ 13 ____________ 14 ____________ 15 ____________

16 ____________ 17 ____________ 18 ____________ 19 ____________ 20 ____________

21 ____________ 22 ____________ 23 ____________ 24 ____________ 25 ____________

QUIZ #16

LESSON 16.4

Identify these states.

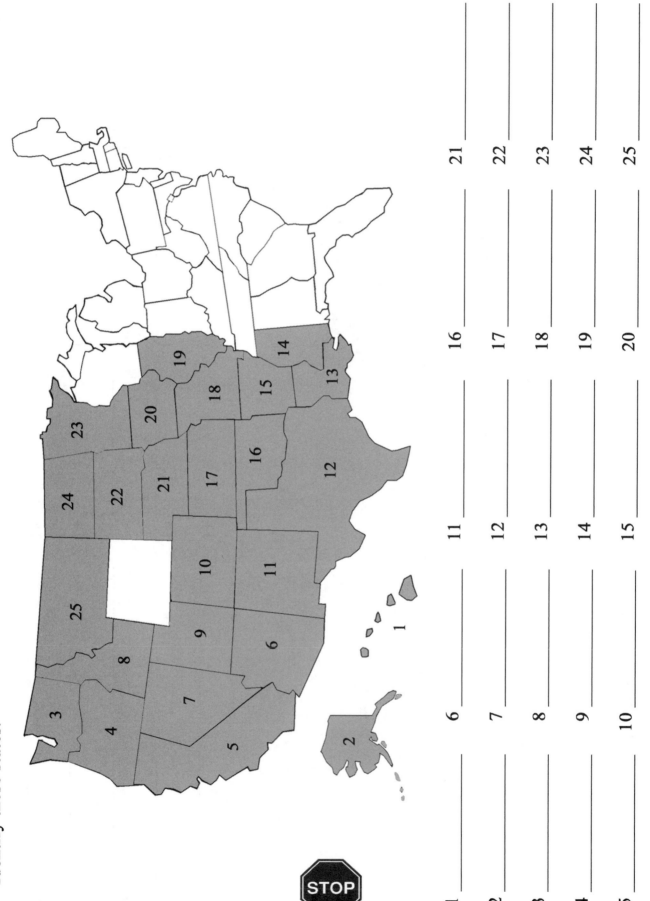

STOP

1 _____
2 _____
3 _____
4 _____
5 _____

6 _____
7 _____
8 _____
9 _____
10 _____

11 _____
12 _____
13 _____
14 _____
15 _____

16 _____
17 _____
18 _____
19 _____
20 _____

21 _____
22 _____
23 _____
24 _____
25 _____

NAME: _____

LESSON 17.1

Date: _____

WISCONSIN

CAPITAL: 1) _____

STATEHOOD: May 29, 1848

Population: 5,479,000
RANK: 18th

Area: 54,314 square miles
RANK: 25th

Milwaukee Madison Green Bay

WHAT WAS THAT? Over the years, Wisconsin has come to be regarded as the UFO capital of the Midwest. Sightings of saucers flying through the air and even balls of light bobbing in nearby lakes have been reported. But, although there's no proof of extraterrestrial life forms existing, who could blame them for visiting Wisconsin if they did? It's a great place to visit if you're in the Milky Way.

30 FACTS

* Wisconsin's motto is simple, yet meaningful: "2) _____."

* Did you know that if you lined up all Wisconsin's streams and rivers, they would stretch around the world?

* In 1854, the Republican Party was founded in Ripon, Wisconsin.

* Famous Wisconsinites include: magician Harry Houdini, circus greats Charles and John Ringling, actor Spencer Tracy, and Supreme Court Justice William Rehnquist.

THE FACTS. With over 44% of Wisconsin's land being owned by farmers, the state has become a huge food producer. In recent years, the Badger State has produced over 2.5 billion pounds of cheese annually. No, not 2.5 million pounds, but 2.5 BILLION. Still, dairy products aren't Wisconsin's only claim to fame. The farming state is also a strong leader in its production of cranberries, ginseng, and beans.

3) Find Wisconsin on this map and shade it in.

4) (True or False) Wisconsin's abbreviation is WN. _____

5) During which year did Wisconsin become a state? _____

6) Wisconsin was the _____ state to join the Union. Hawaii was the 50th.

7) What is the name of Wisconsin's largest city? _____

WISCONSIN

II. What do you remember about Wisconsin? Use the space below.

_____

_____

_____

III. Write the definitions to these words in the spaces provided.

Cheese -- _____

_____

Annual -- _____

_____

IV. Draw a picture of Wisconsin.	V. Connect each word to its picture. WISCONSIN WEST VIRGINIA WASHINGTON
VI. Find Wisconsin on this map.	VII. Unscramble these words. FARREMS _____ CEHESE _____ LIBLIONS _____ CONWISSIN _____

NAME: _____

Date: _____

WYOMING

CAPITAL: 1) _____

STATEHOOD: July 10, 1890

Population: 568,000	Area: 97,105 square miles
RANK: 50th	RANK: 9th

Cheyenne Casper Laramie

OLD FAITHFUL. Yellowstone National Park (America's first national park) is mostly in the state of Wyoming. When people visit, one of their favorite stops is Old Faithful Geyser, just one of a number of hot springs that frequent the park. Erupting from 18 to 21 times a day, the mammoth geyser discharges nearly 7,000 gallons of water each time. The blasts last less than a minute and end with a few puffs of steam.

44 FACTS

* With under 600,000 people, Wyoming is the least-populated 2) _____ in the nation.

* Someone from Wyoming is called a Wyomingite.

* Before the Europeans arrived, the land which was to become Wyoming was teeming with bison.

* In 1906, Wyoming's Devils Tower became our nation's first national monument.

* The coal industry is very important to Wyoming's economy.

THE EQUALITY STATE. You have to hand it to Wyoming; it was the first state to grant women the right to vote in elections. Even as far back as 1869, when Wyoming was a mere territory, 3) _____ had the right to cast ballots.

NOTE: The 19th Amendment to the Constitution was passed in 1920. This guaranteed that women had the same rights as men regarding the right to vote.

4) Find Wyoming on this map and shade it in.

5) What is Wyoming's abbreviation? _____

6) Wyoming's Devils _____ became our nation's first national monument.

7) In what year did Wyoming become a state?

_____

WYOMING

II. What do you remember about Wyoming? Use the space below.

_____

_____

_____

III. Write the definitions to these words in the spaces provided.

Geyser -- _____

_____

Equality -- _____

_____

IV. Draw a picture of Wyoming.	V. Connect each word to its picture.
	WYOMING **WISCONSIN** **WEST VIRGINIA**
VI. Find Wyoming on this map.	**VII. Unscramble these words.** EYQUALIT _____ MENOW _____ TINGOV _____ YOWMING _____

NAME: _____

WASHINGTON, D.C.
Our Nation's Capital Since June 11, 1) _____

DC

Population: 529,000   Area: 68 square miles

To be. President George Washington didn't live in what is now Washington, D.C. He lived in Philadelphia. However, in 1791, he did choose the site that became our new capital. Believe it or not, it was a marshy swamp! By 1800, his plans for a new capital city were complete, and our second president, 2) _____ Adams, moved in.

Fire. Our president lives in the White House. But did you know that the *first* Washington, D.C. home of our Commander-in-Chief was burned to the ground? That's right! During the War of 1812, the British invaded our nation's new capital city and torched the president's home. Fortunately, President James Madison got away.

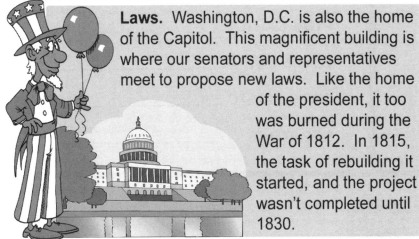

Laws. Washington, D.C. is also the home of the Capitol. This magnificent building is where our senators and representatives meet to propose new laws. Like the home of the president, it too was burned during the War of 1812. In 1815, the task of rebuilding it started, and the project wasn't completed until 1830.

FACTS

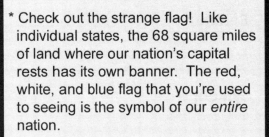

* Check out the strange flag! Like individual states, the 68 square miles of land where our nation's capital rests has its own banner. The red, white, and blue flag that you're used to seeing is the symbol of our *entire* nation.

* Before Washington, D.C. became our nation's capital, New York City held the honor.

* The *D.C.* in Washington, D.C. stands for the District of Columbia, with Columbia referring to Christopher Columbus. *Washington* represents 3) _____ Washington.

Gobble, gobble? Upset with the choice of the bald eagle as our national symbol, Benjamin Franklin said: "The bald eagle is a bird of bad moral character; like those among men who live by robbing, he is generally poor, and often very lousy. The *turkey* is a much more respectable bird and withal a true original native of America." In the end, the eagle's fierce desire to be independent best symbolized the spirit of America.

WASHINGTON, D.C.

II. What do you remember about Washington, D.C.? Use the space below.

_____

_____

_____

III. Write the definitions to these words in the spaces provided.

Senator -- _____

_____

Symbol -- _____

_____

IV. Draw a picture of Washington, D.C.	**V. Connect each word to its picture.** **WASHINGTON, D.C.** **WYOMING** **WISCONSIN**
VI. Find Washington, D.C. on this map.	**VII. Unscramble these words.** **PITALCA TICY** _____ **WITHE OSHUE** _____ **JONH SAMAD** _____ **NESATORS** _____

STOP

Identify these states.

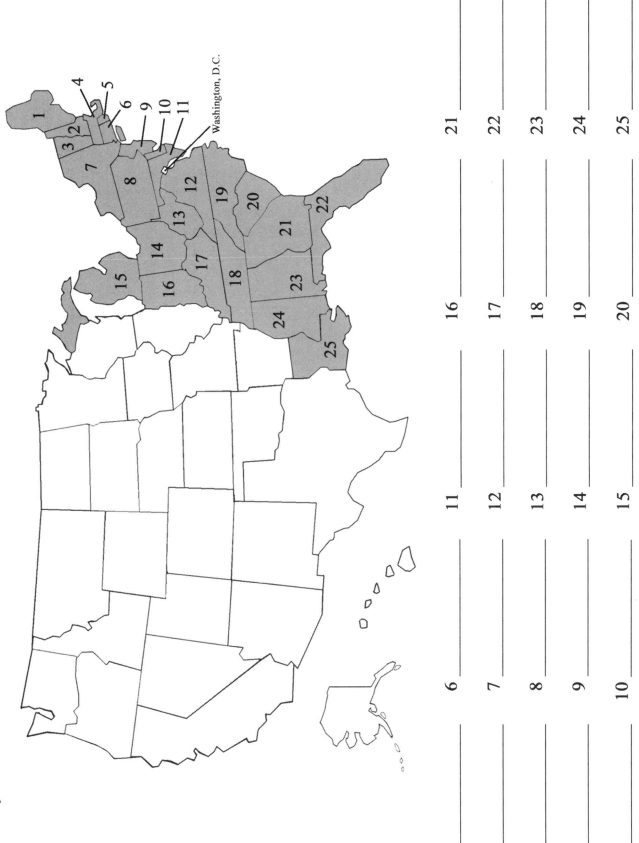

Washington, D.C.

1 _____

2 _____

3 _____

4 _____

5 _____

6 _____

7 _____

8 _____

9 _____

10 _____

11 _____

12 _____

13 _____

14 _____

15 _____

16 _____

17 _____

18 _____

19 _____

20 _____

21 _____

22 _____

23 _____

24 _____

25 _____

QUIZ #17

LESSON 17.4

Identify these states.

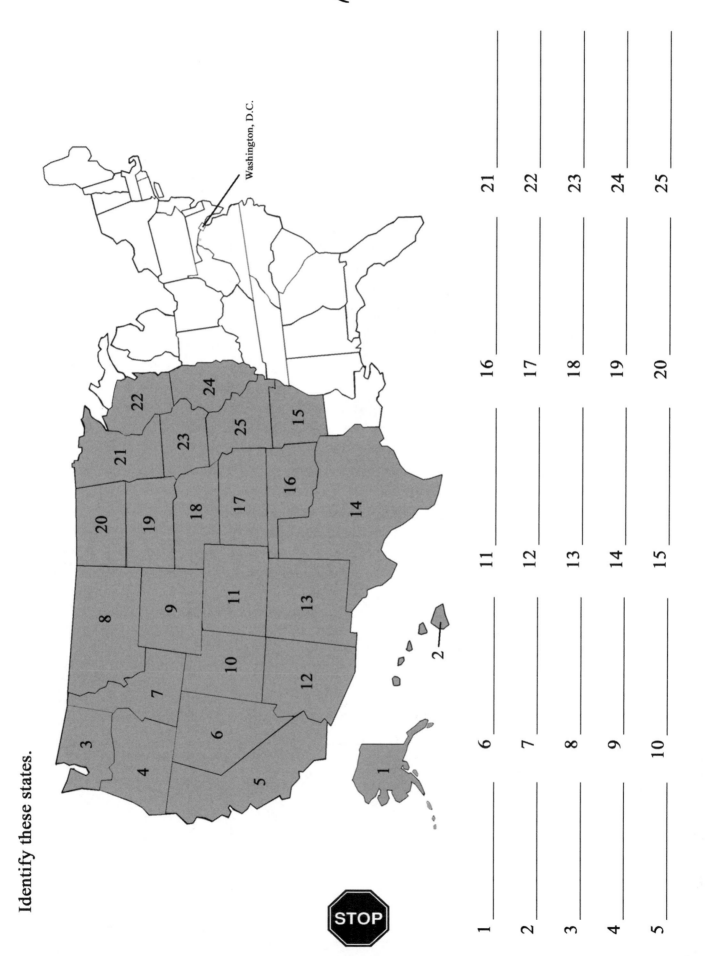

1 _____

2 _____

3 _____

4 _____

5 _____

6 _____

7 _____

8 _____

9 _____

10 _____

11 _____

12 _____

13 _____

14 _____

15 _____

16 _____

17 _____

18 _____

19 _____

20 _____

21 _____

22 _____

23 _____

24 _____

25 _____

Congratulations. You have made it through all fifty states and you still have a few more days to go before this semester is over. So, now that you have some time on your hands, let's play a Geoquiz!

Everytime you take a Geoquiz, you will need to turn to page 5 of *The Star-Spangled State Book.* When you flip over there and look toward the bottom of the page, you'll notice that there are actually **four** Geoquizzes to play. They are: STATES, CAPITALS, BORDERS, and TRIVIA.

This is what you will see.

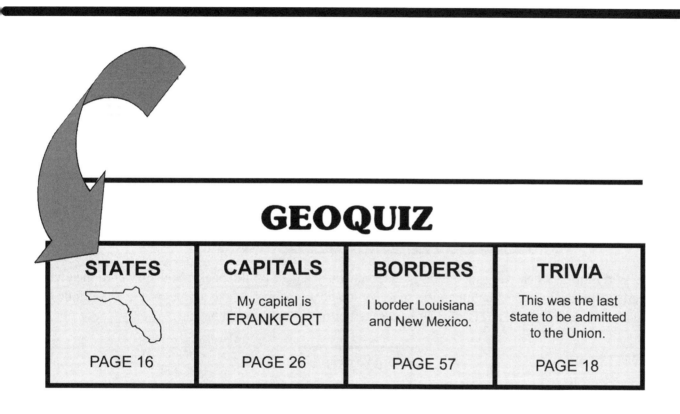

GEOQUIZ

STATES	CAPITALS	BORDERS	TRIVIA
	My capital is FRANKFORT	I border Louisiana and New Mexico.	This was the last state to be admitted to the Union.
PAGE 16	PAGE 26	PAGE 57	PAGE 18

Do you see the four boxes? Good. Now I want you to focus on only one box. Focus on the box that's labeled STATES. It's the one with the arrow pointing to it. **This is your lesson for today. You need to complete the STATES Geoquiz.**

OK, now that you know WHAT you need to do, now it's time to learn HOW to do it. **Keep your focus on the STATES box.** Take a look inside it. Do you see the picture of a state in it? Well, this is your first clue. **Do you remember what state this is?** Is it Florida? Well, when you believe you know the answer, **say your answer out loud and turn to the page number that's shown below the picture.**

This page number will guide you to the correct answer.

When you turn to page 16 of *The Star-Spangled State Book*, you will be on the Florida page.

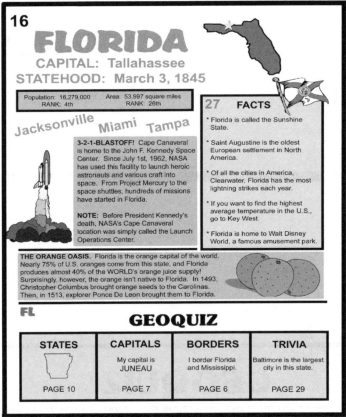

If you said Florida when you saw the first clue, then pat yourself on the back. You answered the clue correctly. But if you said something else, then you made a mistake. Make a note of it and continue by trying to answer the next STATE clue shown at the bottom of the Florida page.

Let's take a look.

Do you know what state this is? Well, like before, say your answer out loud and then flip to the page beneath the clue to see if it takes you to the STATE page that you were expecting. (In this case, you need to turn to page 10.)

Right or wrong, continue to answer all the STATE clues that you come to as you flip the pages through all fifty states. You'll know when you've made it to the end. The STATE box will say "Congratulations."

OK, now that you know how to play, are you ready to try the STATE challenge? Good. Turn to page 5 of *The Star-Spangled State Book* and begin. When you're finished with the Geoquiz, your lesson is over.

NAME: _____

Like yesterday, **take the STATES Geoquiz.**

For each state that you miss, write its name in the area at the bottom of this page. Then review the STATE pages for each state missed.

When you have completed the STATES Geoquiz and reviewed each state that you missed, this lesson is over.

GEOQUIZ

STATES	CAPITALS	BORDERS	TRIVIA
	My capital is **FRANKFORT**	I border Louisiana and New Mexico.	This was the last state to be admitted to the Union.
PAGE 16	PAGE 26	PAGE 57	PAGE 18

STATES TO REVIEW

_____   _____

_____   _____

_____   _____

STUDY DAY!

Tomorrow is your semester exam. To prepare, please review the following lessons and quizzes. Place a checkmark on the line beside each lesson number after you've reviewed it. If you are still having trouble identifying certain states, write their names on the lines at the bottom of this page. Then, review these states one last time.

When you have completed your review, this lesson is over.

LESSON 1.4   _____
LESSON 2.4   _____
LESSON 3.4   _____
LESSON 4.4   _____
LESSON 5.4   _____
LESSON 6.4   _____
LESSON 7.4   _____
LESSON 8.4   _____
LESSON 9.4   _____
LESSON 10.4   _____
LESSON 11.4   _____
LESSON 12.4   _____
LESSON 13.4   _____
LESSON 14.4   _____
LESSON 15.4   _____
LESSON 16.4   _____
LESSON 17.4   _____

STATES TO REVIEW

_____   _____

_____   _____

_____   _____

STOP

EXAM #1

1. Look at this map. Draw a circle around Hawaii and shade in the area that's Alaska.

2. Draw lines to connect each state name to its picture.

Maryland

Rhode Island

Wyoming

Texas

California

Mississippi

Alabama

Delaware

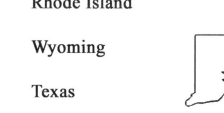

3. Identify these state pictures.

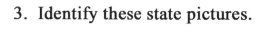 _____

 _____

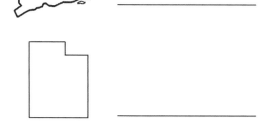 _____

 _____

4. Identify these states.

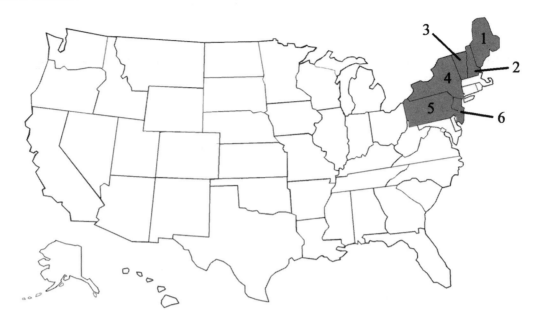

1. _____ 3. _____ 5. _____

2. _____ 4. _____ 6. _____

5. Identify these states.

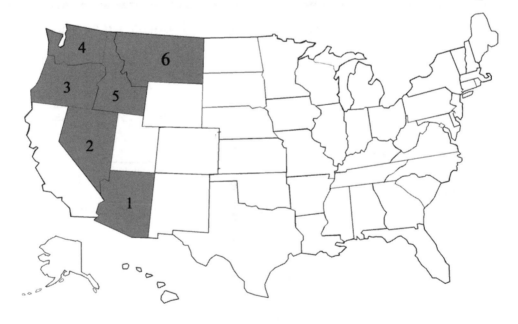

1. _____ 3. _____ 5. _____

2. _____ 4. _____ 6. _____

(CONTINUE ON NEXT PAGE!)

6. Identify these states.

1. _____   3. _____   5. _____

2. _____   4. _____   6. _____

7. Identify these states.

1. _____   3. _____   5. _____

2. _____   4. _____   6. _____

8. Identify these states.

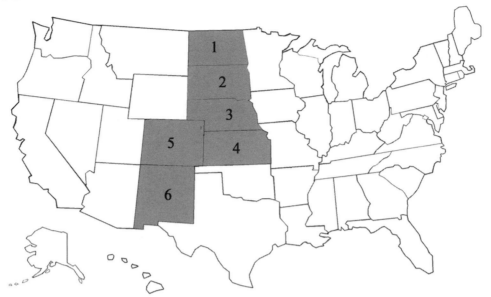

1. _____   3. _____   5. _____

2. _____   4. _____   6. _____

9. Identify these states.

1. _____   3. _____   5. _____

2. _____   4. _____   6. _____

STOP

SECOND SEMESTER

LESSON PLANS
QUIZZES
TESTS

Second Semester

Way to go! You've made it through the first semester. Hopefully, you can identify all 50 states on the map. But if you are still having trouble, keep playing the STATES geoquiz game. It's a big help.

Now, during your second semester, you will need to continue to complete one lesson a day. Four lessons are given each week. (The first three lessons will deal with a specific state. The fourth lesson will be either a quiz or a test.)

If you look at your next lesson (Lesson 19.1), you will notice that it looks a little different than the other ones that you've completed. You will see that most of them are divided into PARTS.

<u>PART 1 will help you to learn about border states.</u> You can use a map if you need to complete this part, but try to do it without a map. One of your goals for the semester is to be able to recall each state's border states from memory.

<u>PART 2 will ask you to identify a state's capital and postal abbreviation.</u> This information can be found in your Star-Spangled State Book. Fill in this section and try to remember each capital and abbreviation. You'll be tested on these in the future.

<u>PART 3 is an exercise in REPETITION, a key to remembering important information.</u> This is a section that you need to complete <u>WITHOUT</u> the use of a map or any of your resources.

At the end of this semester, you will be introduced to two more GEOQUIZZES and you will have an exam. But when the exam is over, I encourage you to keep your Star-Spangled State Book handy. The geoquizzes are an excellent way to refresh your memory when it comes to U.S. Geography!

Can you recite the Pledge of Allegiance?
Start your lessons with this every day!

"I pledge allegiance to the flag of the United States of America. And to the republic for which it stands, one nation, under God, indivisible, with liberty and justice for all."

PART 1

A. Alabama has four border states. Can you identify them?

1. _____
2. _____
3. _____
4. _____

PART 2

A. What is the capital of Alabama? _____

B. What is the abbreviation for Alabama? _____

PART 3

Turn to page 5 of *The Star-Spangled State Book* and take the STATES Geoquiz.

STOP

NAME: _____

PART 1

A. Does Alaska border any states? _____ (If so, list them below.)

1. _____
2. _____
3. _____

PART 2

A. What is the capital of Alaska? _____

B. What is Alaska's abbreviation? _____

PART 3

Alaska borders Canada. Like the United States,
Canada is a <u>country.</u>

A. What country borders Alaska? _____

PART 4

Turn to page 5 of *The Star-Spangled State Book* and take the
<u>STATES</u> Geoquiz.

STOP

PART 1

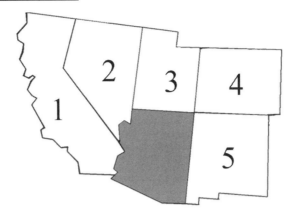

A. Arizona shares its border with five states. Can you identify them?

1. _____
2. _____
3. _____
4. _____
5. _____

PART 2

A. What is the capital of Arizona? _____

B. What is Arizona's abbreviation? _____

PART 3

A. Earlier, you studied Alabama's border states. Without looking at a map, list the four states that share a land border with Alabama.

1. _____
2. _____
3. _____
4. _____

QUIZ #19

1. Draw lines to connect each capital city to its home state.

MONTGOMERY   ARIZONA

PHOENIX   ALABAMA

JUNEAU   ALASKA

_____

2. Draw lines to connect each state to the correct abbreviation. Some of the abbreviations won't be used.

AK

                ALABAMA

AL

AS   ALASKA

AM

                ARIZONA

AZ

_____

3. Do not use a map. In each box below, there is a state that is underlined. Beneath that state, four other states are listed. Of these four states, cross out the one(s) that <u>DO NOT</u> share a border with the underlined state.

ARIZONA	**ALASKA**	**ALABAMA**
NEW MEXICO	NEW MEXICO	TENNESSEE
UTAH	ARIZONA	GEORGIA
CALIFORNIA	CALIFORNIA	FLORIDA
FLORIDA	ALABAMA	OKLAHOMA

NAME: _____

PART 1

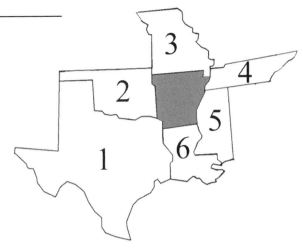

A. Arkansas shares its border with these six states. Can you identify them?

    1. _____

    2. _____

    3. _____

    4. _____

    5. _____

    6. _____

PART 2

A. What is the capital of Arkansas? _____

B. What is abbreviation for Arkansas? _____

PART 3

A. Earlier, you learned about the border states for <u>Alaska</u>. Without looking at a map, answer the following question. How many states border Alaska? _____

STOP

PART 1

A. California shares its border with these three states. Can you identify them?

1. _____
2. _____
3. _____

PART 2

A. What is California's capital? _____

B. What is California's abbreviation? _____

PART 3

A. Earlier, you learned about the border states for <u>Arizona</u>. Without looking at a map, list the five states that share a border with <u>Arizona</u>.

1. _____
2. _____
3. _____
4. _____
5. _____

STOP

PART 1

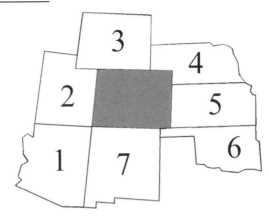

A. Colorado shares its border with these seven states. Can you identify them?

    1. _____
    2. _____
    3. _____
    4. _____
    5. _____
    6. _____
    7. _____

PART 2

A. What is the capital of Colorado? _____

B. What is Colorado's abbreviation? _____

PART 3

A. Earlier, you learned about the border states for <u>Arkansas</u>. Without looking at a map, list the six states that share a border with <u>Arkansas</u>.

    1. _____
    2. _____
    3. _____
    4. _____
    5. _____
    6. _____

STOP

QUIZ #20

1. Draw lines to connect each capital city to its home state.

LITTLE ROCK   CALIFORNIA

DENVER   ARKANSAS

SACRAMENTO   COLORADO

---

2. Draw lines to connect each state to the correct abbreviation. Some of the abbreviations won't be used.

AR

                ARKANSAS

AK

CO

                CALIFORNIA

CR

                COLORADO

CA

---

3. Do not use a map. In each box below, there is a state that is underlined. Beneath that state, four other states are listed. Of these four states, cross out the one(s) that <u>DO NOT</u> share a border with the underlined state.

ARKANSAS	CALIFORNIA	COLORADO
ALASKA	OREGON	WYOMING
TENNESSEE	WASHINGTON	NEW MEXICO
MISSISSIPPI	NEVADA	IOWA
TEXAS	ARIZONA	KENTUCKY

NAME: _____   LESSON 21.1

Date: _____

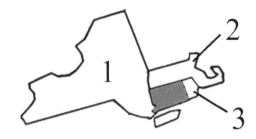

PART 1

A. Connecticut shares its border with these three states. Can you identify them?

1. _____
2. _____
3. _____

PART 2

A. What is the capital of Connecticut? _____

B. What is Connecticut's abbreviation? _____

PART 3

A. Earlier, you learned about the border states for <u>California</u>. Without looking at a map, list the three states that share a border with <u>California</u>.

1. _____
2. _____
3. _____

STOP

PART 1

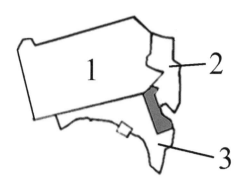

A. Delaware shares its border with these three states. Can you identify them?

1. _____
2. _____
3. _____

PART 2

A. What is the capital of Delaware? _____

B. What is Delaware's abbreviation? _____

PART 3

A. Earlier, you learned about the border states for <u>Colorado</u>. Without looking at a map, list the seven states that share a border with <u>Colorado</u>.

1. _____
2. _____
3. _____
4. _____
5. _____
6. _____
7. _____

STOP

NAME: _____

PART 1

A. Florida shares its border with these two states. Can you identify them?

     1. _____

     2. _____

PART 2

A. What is the capital of Florida? _____

B. What is Florida's abbreviation? _____

A. Earlier, you learned about the border states for <u>Connecticut</u>. Without looking at a map, list the three states that share a border with <u>Connecticut</u>.

PART 3

     1. _____

     2. _____

     3. _____

STOP

QUIZ #21

1. Draw lines to connect each capital city to its home state.

HARTFORD   FLORIDA

TALLAHASSEE   CONNECTICUT

DOVER   DELAWARE

_____

2. Draw lines to connect each state to the correct abbreviation. Some of the abbreviations won't be used.

FL
                            CONNECTICUT
CN

CT   DELAWARE

DE
                            FLORIDA
FA

_____

3. Do not use a map. In each box below, there is a state that is underlined. Beneath that state, four other states are listed. Of these four states, cross out the one(s) that <u>DO NOT</u> share a border with the underlined state.

CONNECTICUT	DELAWARE	FLORIDA
NEW YORK	MARYLAND	NORTH CAROLINA
RHODE ISLAND	PENNSYLVANIA	SOUTH CAROLINA
MAINE	NEW JERSEY	GEORGIA
MASSACHUSETTS	RHODE ISLAND	ALABAMA

PART 1

A. Georgia shares its border with these five states. Can you identify them?

1. _____
2. _____
3. _____
4. _____
5. _____

PART 2

A. What is the capital of Georgia? _____

B. What is Georgia's abbreviation? _____

PART 3

A. Earlier, you learned about the border states for <u>Delaware</u>. Without looking at a map, list the three states that share a border with <u>Delaware</u>.

1. _____
2. _____
3. _____

STOP

PART 1

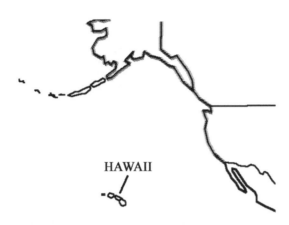

HAWAII

A. Hawaii is a state in the Pacific Ocean. How many states does it border? _____

PART 2

A. What is the capital of Hawaii? _____

B. What is Hawaii's abbreviation? _____

A. Earlier, you learned about the border states for <u>Florida</u>. Without looking at a map, list the two states that share a border with <u>Florida</u>.

PART 3

1. _____
2. _____

PART 1

A. Idaho shares its border with these six states. Can you identify them?

1. _____
2. _____
3. _____
4. _____
5. _____
6. _____

PART 2

A. What is the capital of Idaho? _____

B. What is Idaho's abbreviation? _____

A. Earlier, you learned about the border states for <u>Georgia</u>. Without looking at a map, list the five states that share a border with <u>Georgia</u>.

1. _____
2. _____
3. _____
4. _____
5. _____

PART 3

STOP

NAME: _____

LESSON 22.4

Date: _____

QUIZ #22

1. Draw lines to connect each capital city to its home state.

ATLANTA   GEORGIA

BOISE   HAWAII

HONOLULU   IDAHO

---

2. Draw lines to connect each state to the correct abbreviation. Some of the abbreviations won't be used.

GA
                           GEORGIA
HI

HA   HAWAII

ID
                           IDAHO
IH

---

3. Do not use a map. In each box below, there is a state that is underlined. Beneath that state, four other states are listed. Of these four states, cross out the one(s) that <u>DO NOT</u> share a border with the underlined state.

GEORGIA	**HAWAII**	**IDAHO**
ALABAMA	ALASKA	WASHINGTON
MISSISSIPPI	CALIFORNIA	OREGON
FLORIDA	WASHINGTON	MONTANA
TENNESSEE	GEORGIA	NORTH DAKOTA

NAME: _____

PART 1

A. Illinois shares its border with these five states. Can you identify them?

1. _____
2. _____
3. _____
4. _____
5. _____

PART 2

A. What is the capital of Illinois? _____

B. What is the abbreviation for Illinois? _____

PART 3

A. Earlier, you learned about <u>Hawaii</u>. Without looking at a map, how many states border <u>Hawaii</u>? _____

STOP

PART 1

A. Indiana shares its border with these four states. Can you identify them?

1. _____
2. _____
3. _____
4. _____

PART 2

A. What is the capital of Indiana? _____

B. What is Indiana's abbreviation? _____

A. Earlier, you learned about the border states for <u>Idaho</u>. Without looking at a map, list the five six that share a border with <u>Idaho</u>.

1. _____
2. _____
3. _____
4. _____
5. _____
6. _____

PART 3

STOP

PART 1

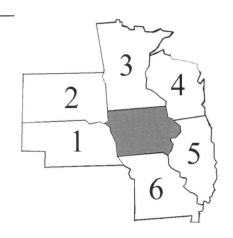

A. Iowa shares its border with these six states. Can you identify them?

1. _____
2. _____
3. _____
4. _____
5. _____
6. _____

PART 2

A. What is the capital of Iowa? _____

B. What is Iowa's abbreviation? _____

A. Earlier, you learned about the border states for <u>Illinois</u>. Without looking at a map, list the five states that share a border with <u>Illinois</u>.

1. _____
2. _____
3. _____
4. _____
5. _____

PART 3

STOP

QUIZ #23

1. Draw lines to connect each capital city to its home state.

INDIANAPOLIS   ILLINOIS

DES MOINES   INDIANA

SPRINGFIELD   IOWA

---

2. Draw lines to connect each state to the correct abbreviation. Some of the abbreviations won't be used.

IN
                    ILLINOIS
IA

ID   INDIANA

IL
                    IOWA
IW

---

3. Do not use a map. In each box below, there is a state that is underlined. Beneath that state, four other states are listed. Of these four states, cross out the one(s) that <u>DO NOT</u> share a border with the underlined state.

ILLINOIS	INDIANA	IOWA
INDIANA	MICHIGAN	NORTH DAKOTA
KENTUCKY	PENNSYLVANIA	SOUTH DAKOTA
MISSOURI	NEW YORK	NEBRASKA
WEST VIRGINIA	OHIO	WISCONSIN

PART 1

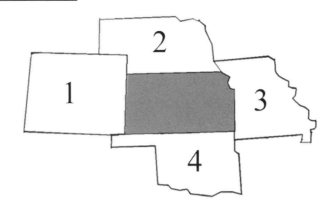

A. Kansas shares its border with these four states. Can you identify them?

1. _____
2. _____
3. _____
4. _____

PART 2

A. What is the capital of Kansas? _____

B. What is the abbreviation of Kansas? _____

A. Earlier, you learned about the border states for <u>Indiana</u>. Without looking at a map, list the four states that share a border with <u>Indiana</u>.

PART 3

1. _____
2. _____
3. _____
4. _____

STOP

PART 1

A. Kentucky shares its border with these seven states. Can you identify them?

1. _____
2. _____
3. _____
4. _____
5. _____
6. _____
7. _____

PART 2

A. What is the capital of Kentucky? _____

B. What is the abbreviation for Kentucky? _____

A. Earlier, you studied the states that border <u>Iowa.</u> Without looking at a map, list six states that border <u>Iowa.</u>

PART 3

1. _____
2. _____
3. _____
4. _____
5. _____
6. _____

STOP

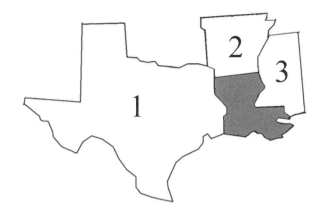

PART 1

A. Louisiana shares its border with these three states. Can you identify them?

    1. _____
    2. _____
    3. _____

PART 2

A. What is the capital of Louisiana? _____

B. What is Louisiana's abbreviation? _____

PART 3

A. Earlier, you learned about the border states for <u>Kansas</u>. Without looking at a map, list the four states that share a border with <u>Kansas</u>.

    1. _____
    2. _____
    3. _____
    4. _____

STOP

QUIZ #24

1. Draw lines to connect each capital city to its home state.

TOPEKA   KANSAS

FRANKFORT   KENTUCKY

BATON ROUGE   LOUISIANA

---

2. Draw lines to connect each state to the correct abbreviation. Some of the abbreviations won't be used.

LA
                KANSAS
KT

KS   KENTUCKY

KY
                LOUISIANA
LO

---

3. Do not use a map. In each box below, there is a state that is underlined. Beneath that state, four other states are listed. Of these four states, cross out the one(s) that DO NOT share a border with the underlined state.

KANSAS	KENTUCKY	LOUISIANA
OKLAHOMA	WEST VIRGINIA	NEW MEXICO
TEXAS	VIRGINIA	TEXAS
COLORADO	OHIO	MISSISSIPPI
MISSOURI	PENNSYLVANIA	ARKANSAS

PART 1

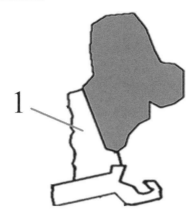

1

A. Maine shares a land border with this one state. Can you identify it?

1. _____

PART 2

A. What is the capital of Maine? _____

B. What is Maine's abbreviation? _____

A. Earlier, you learned about the border states for <u>Kentucky</u>. Without looking at a map, list the seven states that share a border with <u>Kentucky</u>.

PART 3

1. _____
2. _____
3. _____
4. _____
5. _____
6. _____
7. _____

STOP

PART 1

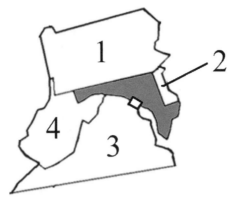

A. Maryland shares its land border with Washington, D.C. and these four states. Can you identify the states?

1. _____
2. _____
3. _____
4. _____

PART 2

A. What is the capital of Maryland? _____

B. What is Maryland's abbreviation? _____

A. Earlier, you learned about the border states for <u>Louisiana</u>. Without looking at a map, list the three states that share a border with <u>Louisiana</u>.

1. _____
2. _____
3. _____

PART 3

STOP

PART 1

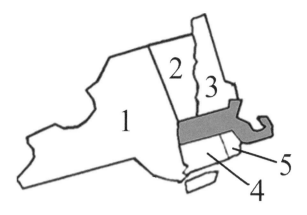

A. Massachusetts shares its border with these five states. Can you identify them?

     1. _____

     2. _____

     3. _____

     4. _____

     5. _____

PART 2

A. What is the capital of Massachusetts? _____

B. What is the abbreviation of Massachusetts? _____

PART 3

A. Earlier, you learned about the border states for <u>Maine</u>. Without looking at a map, list the one state that shares a land border with <u>Maine</u>.

     1. _____

STOP

QUIZ #25

1. Draw lines to connect each capital city to its home state.

BOSTON   MAINE

AUGUSTA   MARYLAND

ANNAPOLIS   MASSACHUSETTS

2. Draw lines to connect each state to the correct abbreviation. Some of the abbreviations won't be used.

MY
                                        MAINE
ME

MA   MARYLAND

MD
                                        MASSACHUSETTS
MT

3. Do not use a map. In each box below, there is a state that is underlined. Beneath that state, four other states are listed. Of these four states, cross out the one(s) that __DO NOT__ share a border with the underlined state.

MAINE	MARYLAND	MASSACHUSETTS
NEW YORK	VIRGINIA	RHODE ISLAND
NEW HAMPSHIRE	DELAWARE	VERMONT
PENNSYLVANIA	NEW YORK	NEW YORK
MARYLAND	WEST VIRGINIA	PENNSYLVANIA

PART 1

A. Michigan shares its land border with these three states. Can you identify them?

1. _____
2. _____
3. _____

PART 2

A. What is the capital of Michigan? _____

B. What is Michigan's abbreviation? _____

PART 3

A. Earlier, you learned about the border states for <u>Maryland</u>. Without looking at a map, list the four states that share a land border with <u>Maryland</u>.

1. _____
2. _____
3. _____
4. _____

STOP

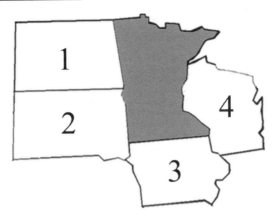

PART 1

A. Minnesota shares its land border with these four states. Can you identify them?

1. _____
2. _____
3. _____
4. _____

PART 2

A. What is the capital of Minnesota? _____

B. What is Minnesota's abbreviation? _____

A. Earlier, you learned about the border states for <u>Massachusetts</u>. Without looking at a map, list the five states that share a border with <u>Massachusetts</u>.

PART 3

1. _____
2. _____
3. _____
4. _____
5. _____

STOP

PART 1

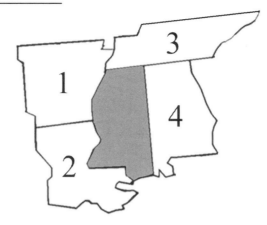

A. Mississippi shares its border with these four states. Can you identify them?

1. _____
2. _____
3. _____
4. _____

PART 2

A. What is the capital of Mississippi? _____

B. What is Mississippi's abbreviation? _____

A. Earlier, you learned about the border states for <u>Michigan</u>. Without looking at a map, list the three states that share a land border with <u>Michigan</u>.

1. _____
2. _____
3. _____

PART 3

STOP

QUIZ #26

1. Draw lines to connect each capital city to its home state.

SAINT PAUL	MICHIGAN
JACKSON	MINNESOTA
LANSING	MISSISSIPPI

_____

2. Draw lines to connect each state to the correct abbreviation. Some of the abbreviations won't be used.

MI

MO
         MICHIGAN

MN
         MINNESOTA

MS
         MISSISSIPPI

MP

_____

3. Do not use a map. In each box below, there is a state that is underlined. Beneath that state, four other states are listed. Of these four states, cross out the one(s) that <u>DO NOT</u> share a border with the underlined state.

MICHIGAN	MINNESOTA	MISSISSIPPI
OHIO	NORTH DAKOTA	TEXAS
INDIANA	SOUTH DAKOTA	LOUISIANA
WISCONSIN	MISSOURI	ARKANSAS
KENTUCKY	IOWA	ALABAMA

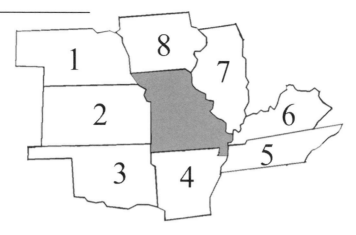

PART 1

A. Missouri shares its border with these eight states. Can you identify them?

1. _____   5. _____

2. _____   6. _____

3. _____   7. _____

4. _____   8. _____

PART 2

A. What is the capital of Missouri? _____

B. What is Missouri's abbreviation? _____

PART 3

A. Earlier, you learned about the border states for <u>Minnesota</u>. Without looking at a map, list the four states that share a land border with <u>Minnesota</u>.

1. _____

2. _____

3. _____

4. _____

STOP

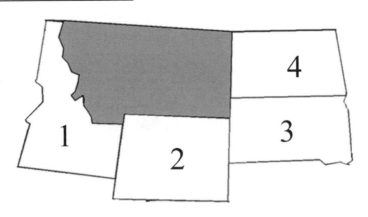

PART 1

A. Montana shares its border with these four states. Can you identify them?

1. _____
2. _____
3. _____
4. _____

PART 2

A. What is the capital of Montana? _____

B. What is Montana's abbreviation? _____

PART 3

A. Earlier, you learned about the border states for <u>Mississippi</u>. Without looking at a map, list four states that share a border with <u>Mississippi</u>.

1. _____
2. _____
3. _____
4. _____

STOP

NAME: _____

LESSON 27.3

Date: _____

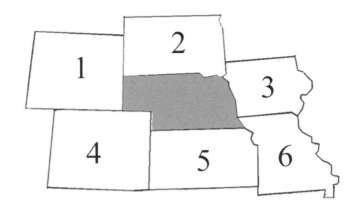

PART 1

A. Nebraska shares its border with these six states. Can you identify them?

1. _____
2. _____
3. _____
4. _____
5. _____
6. _____

PART 2

A. What is the capital of Nebraska? _____

B. What is Nebraska's abbreviation? _____

A. Earlier, you learned about the border states for <u>Missouri</u>. Without looking at a map, list the eight states that share a border with <u>Missouri</u>.

PART 3

1. _____
2. _____
3. _____
4. _____

5. _____
6. _____
7. _____
8. _____

STOP

QUIZ #27

1. Draw lines to connect each capital city to its home state.

HELENA	MISSOURI
LINCOLN	MONTANA
JEFFERSON CITY	NEBRASKA

2. Draw lines to connect each state to the correct abbreviation. Some of the abbreviations won't be used.

MO	
	MISSOURI
MT	
MA	MONTANA
NB	
	NEBRASKA
NE	

3. Do not use a map. In each box below, there is a state that is underlined. Beneath that state, four other states are listed. Of these four states, cross out the one(s) that <u>DO NOT</u> share a border with the underlined state.

MISSOURI	**MONTANA**	**NEBRASKA**
WEST VIRGINIA	NORTH DAKOTA	NORTH DAKOTA
KENTUCKY	SOUTH DAKOTA	SOUTH DAKOTA
ARKANSAS	WASHINGTON	IOWA
LOUISIANA	IDAHO	KANSAS

NAME: _____

LESSON 28.1

Date: _____

PART 1

A. Nevada shares its border with these five states. Can you identify them?

1. _____
2. _____
3. _____
4. _____
5. _____

PART 2

A. What is the capital of Nevada? _____

B. What is Nevada's abbreviation? _____

A. Earlier, you learned about the border states for <u>Montana</u>. Without looking at a map, list the four states that share a border with <u>Montana</u>.

PART 3

1. _____
2. _____
3. _____
4. _____

STOP

PART 1

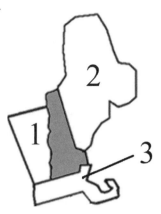

A. New Hampshire shares its border with these three states. Can you identify them?

1. _____
2. _____
3. _____

PART 2

A. What is the capital of New Hampshire? _____

B. What is New Hampshire's abbreviation? _____

PART 3

A. Earlier, you learned about the border states for <u>Nebraska</u>.
Without looking at a map, list the six states that share a border
with <u>Nebraska</u>.

1. _____
2. _____
3. _____
4. _____
5. _____
6. _____

STOP

PART 1

A. New Jersey shares a land border with these three states. Can you identify them?

1. _____
2. _____
3. _____

PART 2

A. What is the capital of New Jersey? _____

B. What is New Jersey's abbreviation? _____

A. Earlier, you learned about the border states for <u>Nevada</u>. Without looking at a map, list the five states that share a border with <u>Nevada</u>.

1. _____
2. _____
3. _____
4. _____
5. _____

PART 3

STOP

QUIZ #28

1. Draw lines to connect each capital city to its home state.

CONCORD   NEVADA

CARSON CITY   NEW HAMPSHIRE

TRENTON   NEW JERSEY

---

2. Draw lines to connect each state to the correct abbreviation. Some of the abbreviations won't be used.

NH

NJ   NEVADA

NA   NEW HAMPSHIRE

NP

NV   NEW JERSEY

---

3. Do not use a map. In each box below, there is a state that is underlined. Beneath that state, four other states are listed. Of these four states, cross out the one(s) that <u>DO NOT</u> share a border with the underlined state.

NEVADA	**NEW HAMPSHIRE**	**NEW JERSEY**
OREGON	NEW YORK	NEW YORK
CALIFORNIA	NEW JERSEY	PENNSYLVANIA
OKLAHOMA	MAINE	VIRGINIA
ARIZONA	NEW MEXICO	WEST VIRGINIA

PART 1

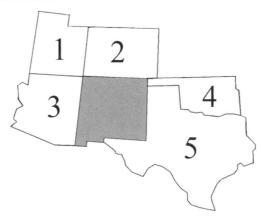

A. New Mexico shares its border with these five states. Can you identify them?

1. _____
2. _____
3. _____
4. _____
5. _____

PART 2

A. What is the capital of New Mexico? _____

B. What is New Mexico's abbreviation? _____

PART 3

A. Earlier, you learned about the border states for <u>New Hampshire</u>. Without looking at a map, list the three states that share a border with <u>New Hampshire</u>.

1. _____
2. _____
3. _____

STOP

NAME: _____

LESSON 29.2

Date: _____

PART 1

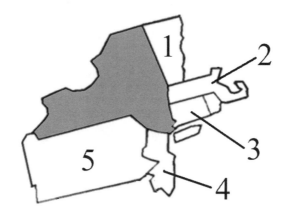

A. New York shares its border with these five states. Can you identify them?

1. _____
2. _____
3. _____
4. _____
5. _____

PART 2

A. What is the capital of New York? _____

B. What is New York's abbreviation? _____

PART 3

A. Earlier, you learned about the border states for <u>New Jersey</u>.
Without looking at a map, list the three states that share a land
border with <u>New Jersey</u>.

1. _____
2. _____
3. _____

PART 1

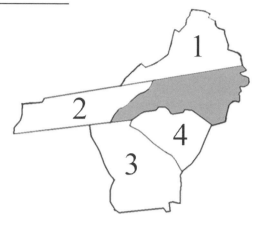

A. North Carolina shares its border with these four states. Can you identify them?

  1. _____
  2. _____
  3. _____
  4. _____

PART 2

A. What is the capital of North Carolina? _____

B. What is North Carolina's abbreviation? _____

A. Earlier, you learned about the border states for <u>New Mexico</u>. Without looking at a map, list the five states that share a border with <u>New Mexico</u>.

PART 3

  1. _____
  2. _____
  3. _____
  4. _____
  5. _____

QUIZ #29

1. Draw lines to connect each capital city to its home state.

ALBANY   NEW MEXICO

RALEIGH   NEW YORK

SANTA FE   NORTH CAROLINA

---

2. Draw lines to connect each state to the correct abbreviation. Some of the abbreviations won't be used.

NO

                NEW MEXICO

NY

NC   NEW YORK

NE

                NORTH CAROLINA

NM

---

3. Do not use a map. In each box below, there is a state that is underlined. Beneath that state, four other states are listed. Of these four states, cross out the one(s) that <u>DO NOT</u> share a border with the underlined state.

NEW MEXICO	NEW YORK	NORTH CAROLINA
TEXAS	NEW JERSEY	SOUTH CAROLINA
ARIZONA	PENNSYLVANIA	FLORIDA
OKLAHOMA	WEST VIRGINIA	VIRGINIA
CALIFORNIA	CALIFORNIA	TENNESSEE

NAME: _____

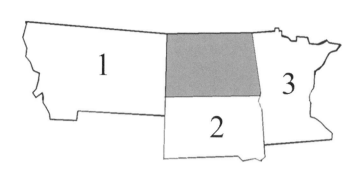

PART 1

A. North Dakota shares its border with these three states. Can you identify them?

1. _____
2. _____
3. _____

PART 2

A. What is the capital of North Dakota? _____

B. What is North Dakota's abbreviation? _____

PART 3

A. Earlier, you learned about the border states for <u>New York</u>. Without looking at a map, list the five states that share a land border with <u>New York</u>.

1. _____
2. _____
3. _____
4. _____
5. _____

STOP

PART 1

A. Ohio shares its border with these five states. Can you identify them?

1. _____
2. _____
3. _____
4. _____
5. _____

PART 2

A. What is the capital of Ohio? _____

B. What is Ohio's abbreviation? _____

PART 3

A. Earlier, you learned about the border states for <u>North Carolina</u>. Without looking at a map, list the four states that share a border with <u>North Carolina</u>.

1. _____
2. _____
3. _____
4. _____

STOP

NAME: _____

PART 1

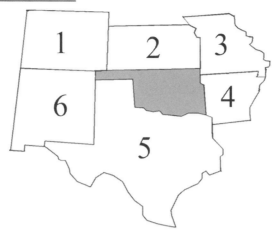

A. Oklahoma shares its border with these six states. Can you identify them?

1. _____
2. _____
3. _____
4. _____
5. _____
6. _____

PART 2

A. What is the capital of Oklahoma? _____

B. What is Oklahoma's abbreviation? _____

PART 3

A. Earlier, you learned about the border states for <u>North Dakota</u>. Without looking at a map, list the three states that share a border with <u>North Dakota</u>.

1. _____
2. _____
3. _____

STOP

QUIZ #30

1. Draw lines to connect each capital city to its home state.

OKLAHOMA CITY   NORTH DAKOTA

BISMARCK   OHIO

COLUMBUS   OKLAHOMA

---

2. Draw lines to connect each state to the correct abbreviation. Some of the abbreviations won't be used.

NK

ND   NORTH DAKOTA

OK   OHIO

OI

OH   OKLAHOMA

---

3. Do not use a map. In each box below, there is a state that is underlined. Beneath that state, four other states are listed. Of these four states, cross out the one(s) that **DO NOT** share a border with the underlined state.

NORTH DAKOTA	**OHIO**	**OKLAHOMA**
MONTANA	PENNSYLVANIA	CALIFORNIA
SOUTH DAKOTA	MICHIGAN	LOUISIANA
MICHIGAN	WEST VIRGINIA	TEXAS
OREGON	VIRGINIA	ARKANSAS

NAME: _____

LESSON 31.1

Date: _____

PART 1

A. Oregon shares its border with these four states. Can you identify them?

1. _____
2. _____
3. _____
4. _____

PART 2

A. What is the capital of Oregon? _____

B. What is Oregon's abbreviation? _____

PART 3

A. Earlier, you learned about the border states for <u>Ohio</u>. Without looking at a map, list the five states that share a border with <u>Ohio</u>.

1. _____
2. _____
3. _____
4. _____
5. _____

STOP

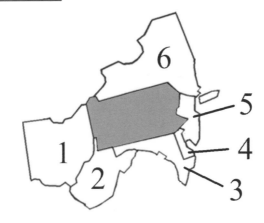

PART 1

A. Pennsylvania shares its border with these six states. Can you identify them?

1. _____
2. _____
3. _____
4. _____
5. _____
6. _____

PART 2

A. What is the capital of Pennsylvania? _____

B. What is Pennsylvania's abbreviation? _____

A. Earlier, you learned about the border states for <u>Oklahoma</u>.
Without looking at a map, list the six states that share a border
with <u>Oklahoma</u>.

1. _____
2. _____
3. _____
4. _____
5. _____
6. _____

PART 3

STOP

PART 1

A. Rhode Island shares its land border with these two states. Can you identify them?

1. _____

2. _____

PART 2

A. What is the capital of Rhode Island? _____

B. What is Rhode Island's abbreviation? _____

A. Earlier, you learned about the border states for <u>Oregon</u>. Without looking at a map, list the four states that share a border with <u>Oregon</u>.

PART 3

1. _____

2. _____

3. _____

4. _____

QUIZ #31

1. Draw lines to connect each capital city to its home state.

HARRISBURG   OREGON

SALEM   PENNSYLVANIA

PROVIDENCE   RHODE ISLAND

_____

2. Draw lines to connect each state to the correct abbreviation. Some of the abbreviations won't be used.

OR

                       OREGON

RH

RI   PENNSYLVANIA

PA

                       RHODE ISLAND

ON

_____

3. Do not use a map. In each box below, there is a state that is underlined. Beneath that state, four other states are listed. Of these four states, cross out the one(s) that <u>DO NOT</u> share a border with the underlined state.

OREGON	PENNSYLVANIA	RHODE ISLAND
CALIFORNIA	NEW YORK	MASSACHUSETTS
WASHINGTON	OHIO	MAINE
IDAHO	MAINE	CONNECTICUT
ARIZONA	MARYLAND	MARYLAND

NAME: _____

PART 1

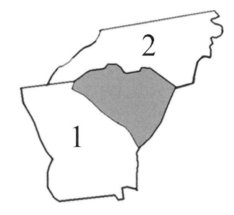

A. South Carolina shares its border with these two states. Can you identify them?

1. _____

2. _____

PART 2

A. What is the capital of South Carolina? _____

B. What is South Carolina's abbreviation? _____

A. Earlier, you learned about the border states for <u>Pennsylvania</u>. Without looking at a map, list the six states that share a border with <u>Pennsylvania</u>.

PART 3

1. _____

2. _____

3. _____

4. _____

5. _____

6. _____

STOP

NAME: _____

Date: _____

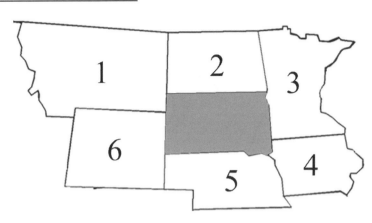

PART 1

A. South Dakota shares its border with these six states. Can you identify them?

1. _____
2. _____
3. _____
4. _____
5. _____
6. _____

PART 2

A. What is the capital of South Dakota? _____

B. What is South Dakota's abbreviation? _____

PART 3

A. Earlier, you learned about the border states for <u>Rhode Island</u>. Without looking at a map, list the two states that share a land border with <u>Rhode Island</u>.

1. _____
2. _____

PART 1

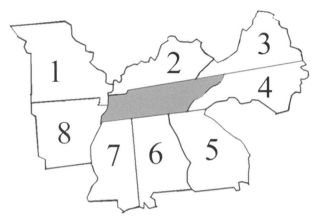

A. Tennessee shares its border with these eight states. Can you identify them?

1. _____   5. _____
2. _____   6. _____
3. _____   7. _____
4. _____   8. _____

PART 2

A. What is the capital of Tennessee? _____

B. What is Tennessee's abbreviation? _____

PART 3

A. Earlier, you learned about the border states for <u>South Carolina</u>.
Without looking at a map, list the two states that share a border with
<u>South Carolina</u>.

1. _____
2. _____

QUIZ #32

1. Draw lines to connect each capital city to its home state.

COLUMBIA   SOUTH CAROLINA

NASHVILLE   SOUTH DAKOTA

PIERRE   TENNESSEE

---

2. Draw lines to connect each state to the correct abbreviation. Some of the abbreviations won't be used.

SD
                            SOUTH CAROLINA
SC

SA   SOUTH DAKOTA

TE
                            TENNESSEE
TN

---

3. Do not use a map. In each box below, there is a state that is underlined. Beneath that state, four other states are listed. Of these four states, cross out the one(s) that <u>DO NOT</u> share a border with the underlined state.

SOUTH CAROLINA	SOUTH DAKOTA	TENNESSEE
NORTH CAROLINA	MICHIGAN	KENTUCKY
VIRGINIA	NORTH DAKOTA	VIRGINIA
GEORGIA	MINNESOTA	NORTH CAROLINA
LOUISIANA	MONTANA	SOUTH CAROLINA

PART 1

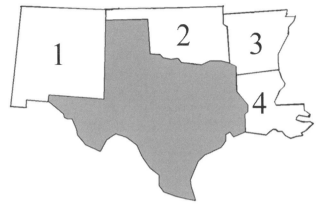

A. Texas shares its border with these four states. Can you identify them?

1. _____
2. _____
3. _____
4. _____

PART 2

A. What is the capital of Texas? _____

B. What is the abbreviation for Texas? _____

PART 3

A. Earlier, you learned about the border states for <u>South Dakota</u>. Without looking at a map, list the six states that share a border with <u>South Dakota</u>.

1. _____
2. _____
3. _____
4. _____
5. _____
6. _____

STOP

NAME: _____

LESSON 33.2

Date: _____

PART 1

A. Utah shares its border with these six states. Can you identify them?

1. _____
2. _____
3. _____
4. _____
5. _____
6. _____

PART 2

A. What is the capital of Utah? _____

B. What is Utah's abbreviation? _____

PART 3

A. Earlier, you learned about the border states for <u>Tennessee</u>.
Without looking at a map, list the eight states that share a
border with <u>Tennessee</u>.

1. _____   5. _____
2. _____   6. _____
3. _____   7. _____
4. _____   8. _____

PART 1

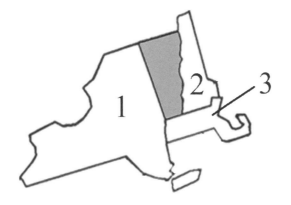

A. Vermont shares its border with these three states. Can you identify them?

1. _____
2. _____
3. _____

PART 2

A. What is the capital of Vermont? _____

B. What is Vermont's abbreviation? _____

A. Earlier, you learned about the border states for <u>Texas</u>. Without looking at a map, list the four states that share a border with <u>Texas</u>.

PART 3

1. _____
2. _____
3. _____
4. _____

STOP

QUIZ #33

1. Draw lines to connect each capital city to its home state.

SALT LAKE CITY	TEXAS
AUSTIN	UTAH
MONTPELIER	VERMONT

---

2. Draw lines to connect each state to the correct abbreviation. Some of the abbreviations won't be used.

TE

TX   TEXAS

VN   UTAH

VT

UT   VERMONT

---

3. Do not use a map. In each box below, there is a state that is underlined. Beneath that state, four other states are listed. Of these four states, cross out the one(s) that <u>DO NOT</u> share a border with the underlined state.

TEXAS	**UTAH**	**VERMONT**
LOUISIANA	IDAHO	NEW YORK
OKLAHOMA	NORTH DAKOTA	NEW HAMPSHIRE
NEW MEXICO	WASHINGTON	MASSACHUSETTS
ARIZONA	COLORADO	MAINE

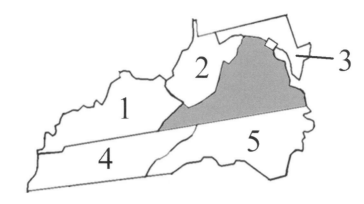

PART 1

A. Virginia shares its border with these five states. Can you identify them?

1. _____
2. _____
3. _____
4. _____
5. _____

PART 2

A. What is the capital of Virginia? _____

B. What is Virginia's abbreviation? _____

PART 3

A. Earlier, you learned about the border states for <u>Utah</u>. Without looking at a map, list the six states that share a border with <u>Utah</u>.

1. _____
2. _____
3. _____
4. _____
5. _____
6. _____

STOP

PART 1

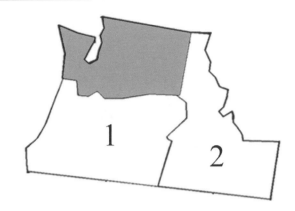

A. Washington shares its border with these two states. Can you identify them?

1. _____
2. _____

PART 2

A. What is the capital of Washington? _____

B. What is Washington's abbreviation? _____

PART 3

A. Earlier, you learned about the border states for <u>Vermont</u>. Without looking at a map, list the three states that share a border with <u>Vermont</u>.

1. _____
2. _____
3. _____

NAME: _____

LESSON 34.3

Date: _____

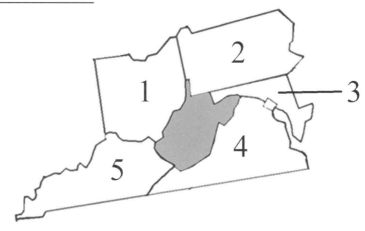

PART 1

A. West Virginia shares its border with these five states. Can you identify them?

1. _____
2. _____
3. _____
4. _____
5. _____

PART 2

A. What is the capital of West Virginia? _____

B. What is West Virginia's abbreviation? _____

A. Earlier, you learned about the border states for Virginia. Without looking at a map, list the five states that share a border with Virginia.

PART 3

1. _____
2. _____
3. _____
4. _____
5. _____

STOP

QUIZ #34

1. Draw lines to connect each capital city to its home state.

RICHMOND   VIRGINIA

CHARLESTON   WASHINGTON

OLYMPIA   WEST VIRGINIA

_____

2. Draw lines to connect each state to the correct abbreviation. Some of the abbreviations won't be used.

VI

VA
                            VIRGINIA

WT   WASHINGTON

WV
                            WEST VIRGINIA

WA

_____

3. Do not use a map. In each box below, there is a state that is underlined. Beneath that state, four other states are listed. Of these four states, cross out the one(s) that DO NOT share a border with the underlined state.

VIRGINIA	WASHINGTON	WEST VIRGINIA
MARYLAND	ALASKA	OHIO
WEST VIRGINIA	OREGON	KENTUCKY
NORTH CAROLINA	CALIFORNIA	VIRGINIA
SOUTH CAROLINA	IDAHO	ILLINOIS

NAME: _____

PART 1

A. Wisconsin shares its border with these four states. Can you identify them?

1. _____
2. _____
3. _____
4. _____

PART 2

A. What is the capital of Wisconsin? _____

B. What is Wisconsin's abbreviation? _____

PART 3

A. Earlier, you learned about the border states for <u>Washington</u>.
Without looking at a map, list the two states that share a border
with <u>Washington</u>.

1. _____
2. _____

STOP

PART 1

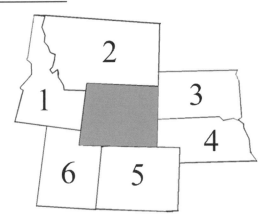

A. Wyoming shares its border with these six states. Can you identify them?

1. _____
2. _____
3. _____
4. _____
5. _____
6. _____

PART 2

A. What is the capital of Wyoming? _____

B. What is Wyoming's abbreviation? _____

A. Earlier, you learned about the border states for <u>West Virginia</u>. Without looking at a map, list the five states that share a border with <u>West Virginia.</u>

PART 3

1. _____
2. _____
3. _____
4. _____
5. _____

STOP

PART 1

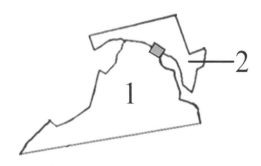

A. Washington, D.C. shares its border with these two states. Can you identify them?

      1. _____

      2. _____

PART 2

A. Is Washington, D.C. a state? _____

B. Washington, D.C. is the capital of what country? _____
_____

PART 3

A. Earlier, you learned about the border states for <u>Wisconsin.</u>
Without looking at a map, list the four states that share a
border with <u>Wisconsin.</u>

      1. _____

      2. _____

      3. _____

      4. _____

STOP

QUIZ #35

1. Draw lines to connect each capital city to its home state.

MADISON   WISCONSIN

CHEYENNE   WYOMING

2. Draw lines to connect each state to the correct abbreviation. Some of the abbreviations won't be used.

WI

                   WISCONSIN

WN

WO   WYOMING

WY

3. Do not use a map. In each box below, there is a state that is underlined. Beneath that state, four other states are listed. Of these four states, cross out the one(s) that <u>DO NOT</u> share a border with the underlined state.

WISCONSIN	**WYOMING**
MICHIGAN	COLORADO
NEW YORK	MONTANA
KENTUCKY	WASHINGTON
ILLINOIS	TEXAS

4. Washington, D.C. borders two states. Name them. _____
   and _____ .

Congratulations, there are only a few days left before this course is finished. Now that you've been introduced to the capitals, abbreviations, and border states for all fifty states (and Washington, D.C.), you are able to play two more GEOQUIZ games.

Remember the STATES geoquiz game? (Hopefully, you're able to identify all the pictures of the states.) Well, like you did with the STATES game, I want you to turn to page 5 of *The Star-Spangled State Book*. But this time, instead of playing the STATES game, I want you to complete the following two tasks.

PART 1   Complete the <u>CAPITALS</u> Geoquiz!

PART 2   Complete the <u>BORDERS</u> Geoquiz!

PART 1

Fill in the blanks with the correct state abbreviations.

_____ Alabama	_____ Louisiana	_____ Ohio
_____ Alaska	_____ Maine	_____ Oklahoma
_____ Arizona	_____ Maryland	_____ Oregon
_____ Arkansas	_____ Massachusetts	_____ Pennsylvania
_____ California	_____ Michigan	_____ Rhode Island
_____ Colorado	_____ Minnesota	_____ South Carolina
_____ Connecticut	_____ Mississippi	_____ South Dakota
_____ Delaware	_____ Missouri	_____ Tennessee
_____ Florida	_____ Montana	_____ Texas
_____ Georgia	_____ Nebraska	_____ Utah
_____ Hawaii	_____ Nevada	_____ Vermont
_____ Idaho	_____ New Hampshire	_____ Virginia
_____ Illinois	_____ New Jersey	_____ Washington
_____ Indiana	_____ New Mexico	_____ West Virginia
_____ Iowa	_____ New York	_____ Wisconsin
_____ Kansas	_____ North Carolina	_____ Wyoming
_____ Kentucky	_____ North Dakota	

PART 2

Complete the <u>CAPITALS</u> Geoquiz!

PART 1

Fill in the blanks with the correct state abbreviations.

_____ Alabama
_____ Alaska
_____ Arizona
_____ Arkansas
_____ California
_____ Colorado
_____ Connecticut
_____ Delaware
_____ Florida
_____ Georgia
_____ Hawaii
_____ Idaho
_____ Illinois
_____ Indiana
_____ Iowa
_____ Kansas
_____ Kentucky

_____ Louisiana
_____ Maine
_____ Maryland
_____ Massachusetts
_____ Michigan
_____ Minnesota
_____ Mississippi
_____ Missouri
_____ Montana
_____ Nebraska
_____ Nevada
_____ New Hampshire
_____ New Jersey
_____ New Mexico
_____ New York
_____ North Carolina
_____ North Dakota

_____ Ohio
_____ Oklahoma
_____ Oregon
_____ Pennsylvania
_____ Rhode Island
_____ South Carolina
_____ South Dakota
_____ Tennessee
_____ Texas
_____ Utah
_____ Vermont
_____ Virginia
_____ Washington
_____ West Virginia
_____ Wisconsin
_____ Wyoming

PART 2

Complete the __CAPITALS__ Geoquiz!

EXAM #2

1. **Fill in the blanks with the correct state abbreviations.**

_____ Alabama	_____ Louisiana	_____ Ohio
_____ Alaska	_____ Maine	_____ Oklahoma
_____ Arizona	_____ Maryland	_____ Oregon
_____ Arkansas	_____ Massachusetts	_____ Pennsylvania
_____ California	_____ Michigan	_____ Rhode Island
_____ Colorado	_____ Minnesota	_____ South Carolina
_____ Connecticut	_____ Mississippi	_____ South Dakota
_____ Delaware	_____ Missouri	_____ Tennessee
_____ Florida	_____ Montana	_____ Texas
_____ Georgia	_____ Nebraska	_____ Utah
_____ Hawaii	_____ Nevada	_____ Vermont
_____ Idaho	_____ New Hampshire	_____ Virginia
_____ Illinois	_____ New Jersey	_____ Washington
_____ Indiana	_____ New Mexico	_____ West Virginia
_____ Iowa	_____ New York	_____ Wisconsin
_____ Kansas	_____ North Carolina	_____ Wyoming
_____ Kentucky	_____ North Dakota	

2. What is the abbreviation for Washington, D.C.? _____

3. What two states border Washington, D.C.? _____ and

_____ .

4. What is the capital of The United States of America? _____

_____

5. The United States is made up of how many states? _____

EXAM #2

6. Match each capital to its state.

_____ Alaska   A. Frankfort

_____ California   B. Madison

_____ Delaware   C. Columbus

_____ Hawaii   D. Providence

_____ Illinois   E. Sacramento

_____ Kentucky   F. Trenton

_____ Louisiana   G. Honolulu

_____ Minnesota   H. Juneau

_____ New Jersey   I. Baton Rouge

_____ North Dakota   J. Dover

_____ Ohio   K. Bismarck

_____ Rhode Island   L. Austin

_____ Texas   M. Saint Paul

_____ Washington   N. Olympia

_____ Wisconsin   O. Springfield

7. In each box, there are some states. These states share a border with one other state. Write the name of that state on the blank line in the box.

————————	————————	————————
OREGON	NEW YORK	ALABAMA
NEVADA	MARYLAND	FLORIDA
ARIZONA	OHIO	NORTH CAROLINA
	WEST VIRGINIA	SOUTH CAROLINA

————————	————————	————————
TEXAS	WYOMING	KENTUCKY
COLORADO	COLORADO	NORTH CAROLINA
MISSOURI	IOWA	ALABAMA
ARKANSAS	MISSOURI	ARKANSAS

————————	————————	————————
CONNECTICUT	MINNESOTA	ILLINOIS
RHODE ISLAND	MICHIGAN	TENNESSEE
NEW YORK	IOWA	ARKANSAS
NEW HAMPSHIRE	ILLINOIS	KANSAS

EXAM #2

LESSON 36.4

Identify these states.

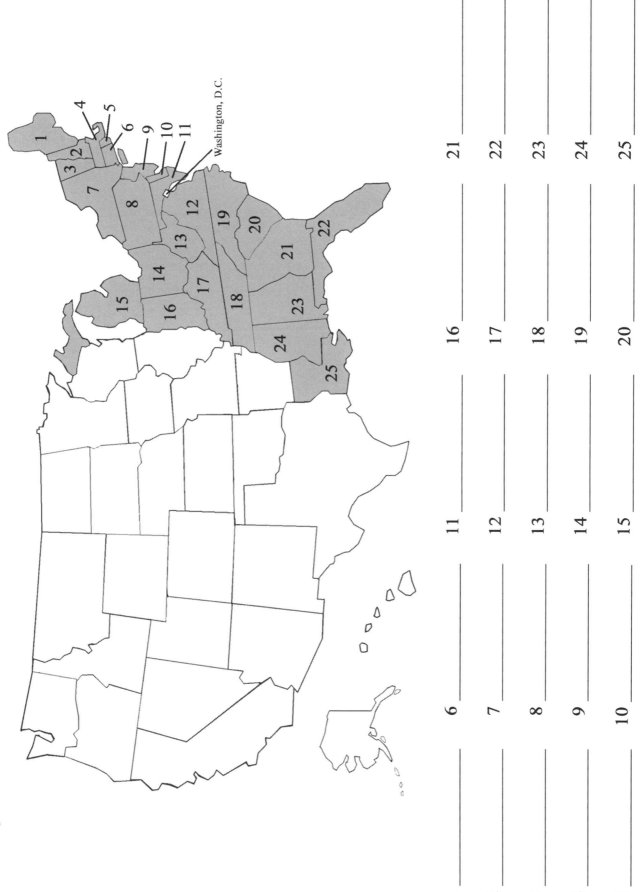

Washington, D.C.

1 _____

2 _____

3 _____

4 _____

5 _____

6 _____

7 _____

8 _____

9 _____

10 _____

11 _____

12 _____

13 _____

14 _____

15 _____

16 _____

17 _____

18 _____

19 _____

20 _____

21 _____

22 _____

23 _____

24 _____

25 _____

EXAM #2

Identify these states.

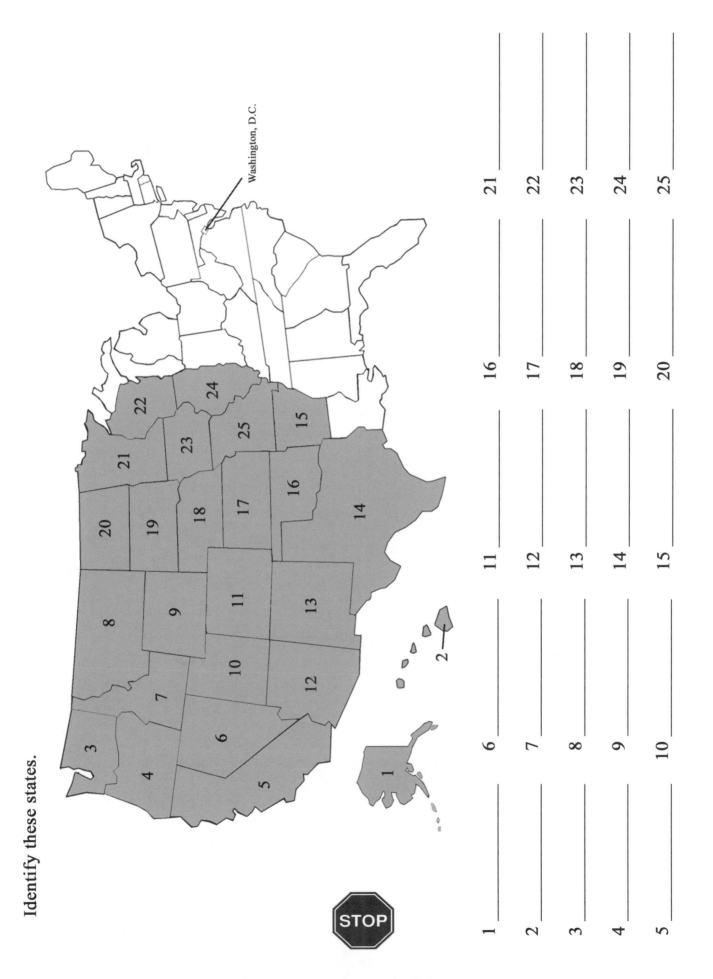

STOP

1 _____

2 _____

3 _____

4 _____

5 _____

6 _____

7 _____

8 _____

9 _____

10 _____

11 _____

12 _____

13 _____

14 _____

15 _____

16 _____

17 _____

18 _____

19 _____

20 _____

21 _____

22 _____

23 _____

24 _____

25 _____

ANSWER
KEYS

AND
REPORT CARD

NAME: _____

LESSON 1.4
Date: _____

QUIZ #1

1. Here is a map of the world. Color (or shade in) the area that is the United States of America.

"Don't forget about the island!"

2. Draw lines to connect each state name to its picture.

ARIZONA

ALASKA

ALABAMA

3. These three states are all scrambled up. Correctly spell them in the space provided.

ZONARIA   *ARIZONA*

SLAAKA   *ALASKA*

AMABALA   *ALABAMA*

LESSON 1.4

QUIZ #1

4. Three states are listed below. Color (or shade in) each of these states on the map. Then draw lines to connect each state name to its colored area.

Alaska   Arizona   Alabama

SECTION 5

A. The United States of America is divided into how many states?   *50*

B. What is a border? *A LINE THAT SETS BOUNDARIES.*

C. I haven't mentioned this before, but there is a special name for the 48 states that are clustered together. Together, these 48 states are called the *Continental United States.* Now, with that in mind, which two states are NOT part of the *Continental United States*?   *ALASKA*   and   *HAWAII* .

STOP

NAME: _____

LESSON 2.4
Date: _____

QUIZ #2

1. Three states are listed below. Color (or shade in) each of these states on the map. Then draw lines to connect each state name to its colored area.

California   Colorado   Arkansas

2. You should still remember these! Draw lines to connect each state name to its picture.

ARIZONA

ALASKA

ALABAMA

3. These three states are all scrambled up. Correctly spell them in the space provided.

IFORCALINA   *CALIFORNIA*

SLAAKA   *ALASKA*

SASARKAN   *ARKANSAS*

QUIZ #2   LESSON 2.4

4. Correctly label each of the following state pictures. The last state begins with the letter <u>C</u>.

 ALASKA   *ARKANSAS*

 ALABAMA   *CALIFORNIA*

 ARIZONA   *COLORADO*

CHECKPOINT!

At this point you should be able to find SIX states on the map: **Alabama, Alaska, Arizona, Arkansas, California, and Colorado.**

Are you able to find them? I bet you can. But if you can't, don't worry. Just review these lessons until you're able. Between me and you, repetition is key!

Oh, and one more thing. Do you know what Arizona and California have in common? They border one another! Keep learning and in a few weeks, you might be able to close your eyes and name ALL the states that border California. And not just California, but any state!

Remember: U.S. Geography isn't hard; it's just a fifty-piece puzzle.

 STOP

QUIZ #3

NAME: _____ LESSON 3.4
Date: _____

1. Three states are listed below. Color (or shade in) each of these states on the map. Then draw lines to connect each state name to its colored area.

Florida   Delaware   Connecticut

2. You should still remember these! Draw lines to connect each state name to its picture.

COLORADO

CALIFORNIA

ARKANSAS

3. These three states are all scrambled up. Correctly spell them in the space provided.

a. ICUTCONNECT   *CONNECTICUT*

b. AMALABA   *ALABAMA*

c. LAREWADE   *DELAWARE*

QUIZ #3

LESSON 3.4

4. Correctly label these pictures.

ALASKA   *ALABAMA*

ARKANSAS   *CONNECTICUT*

FLORIDA   *DELAWARE*

5. Identify these states.

1. *CALIFORNIA*   3. *ALABAMA*   5. *FLORIDA*
2. *ARIZONA*   4. *ARKANSAS*   6. *ALASKA*

STOP

QUIZ #4

NAME: _____ LESSON 4.4
Date: _____

1. Three states are listed below. Color (or shade in) each of these states on the map. Then draw lines to connect each state name to its colored area.

Hawaii   Idaho   Georgia

2. You should still remember these! Draw lines to connect each state name to its picture.

ARIZONA

ALABAMA

DELAWARE

3. These three states are all scrambled up. Correctly spell them in the space provided.

AWARDELE   *DELAWARE*

ADIFLOR   *FLORIDA*

ICUTCONNECT   *CONNECTICUT*

QUIZ #4

LESSON 4.4

Correctly label these six state pictures.

CONNECTICUT   *ARKANSAS*

CALIFORNIA   *DELAWARE*

HAWAII   *FLORIDA*

Identify these states.

1 *ARIZONA*   2 *COLORADO*   3 *ALABAMA*
4 *GEORGIA*   5 *CONNECTICUT*   6 *HAWAII*

STOP

QUIZ #5

NAME: _____

LESSON 5.4

Date: _____

1. Three states are listed below. Color (or shade in) each of these states on the map. Then draw lines to connect each state name to its colored area.

Iowa   Illinois   Indiana

2. See if you can remember these! Draw lines to connect each state name to its picture.

COLORADO

IDAHO

ARIZONA

3. These three states are all scrambled up. Correctly spell them in the space provided.

HOIDA   *IDAHO*

OWIA   *IOWA*

ANADINI   *INDIANA*

QUIZ #5

LESSON 5.4

Correctly label these six state pictures. The last one begins with the letter C.

FLORIDA   *DELAWARE*

ALASKA   *CONNECTICUT*

HAWAII   *COLORADO*

Identify these states.

| 1 | *IDAHO* | 2 | *ARKANSAS* | 3 | *GEORGIA* |
| 4 | *IOWA* | 5 | *ILLINOIS* | 6 | *INDIANA* |

STOP

QUIZ #6

NAME: _____

LESSON 6.4

Date: _____

1. Three states are listed below. Color (or shade in) each of these states on the map. Then draw lines to connect each state name to its colored area.

Kansas   Louisiana   Kentucky

2. See if you can remember these! Draw lines to connect each state name to its picture.

INDIANA

IOWA

ILLINOIS

3. Here are a few more to try! Draw lines to connect each state name to its picture.

CONNECTICUT

IDAHO

GEORGIA

QUIZ #6

LESSON 6.4

Identify these states.

| 1 | *ALASKA* | 2 | *CALIFORNIA* | 3 | *ARIZONA* |
| 4 | *IDAHO* | 5 | *COLORADO* | 6 | *HAWAII* |

Identify these states.

| 1 | *CONNECTICUT* | 2 | *DELAWARE* | 3 | *KANSAS* |
| 4 | *IOWA* | 5 | *ILLINOIS* | 6 | *INDIANA* |

STOP

QUIZ #7

NAME: _____ LESSON 7.4

Date: _____

1. Three states are listed below. Color (or shade in) each of these states on the map. Then draw lines to connect each state name to its colored area.

Maryland   Massachusetts   Maine

2. See if you can remember these! Draw lines to connect each state name to its picture.

CONNECTICUT

KANSAS

ALABAMA

3. Here are a few more to try! Draw lines to connect each state name to its picture.

INDIANA

ILLINOIS

KENTUCKY

QUIZ #7

LESSON 7.4

Identify these states.

| 1 | *CALIFORNIA* | 2 | *ARIZONA* | 3 | *MAINE* |
| 4 | *MASSACHUSETTS* | 5 | *CONNECTICUT* | 6 | *MARYLAND* |

Identify these states.

1	*IOWA*	2	*ILLINOIS*	3	*INDIANA*
4	*KENTUCKY*	5	*FLORIDA*	6	*GEORGIA*
7	*MISSISSIPPI*	8	*ARKANSAS*	9	*KANSAS*

STOP

QUIZ #8

NAME: _____ LESSON 8.4

Date: _____

1. Three states are listed below. Color (or shade in) each of these states on the map. Then draw lines to connect each state name to its colored area.

Minnesota   Michigan   Mississippi

2. See if you can remember these! Draw lines to connect each state name to its picture.

MASSACHUSETTS

ALABAMA

MISSISSIPPI

3. Here are a few more to try! Draw lines to connect each state name to its picture.

IOWA

LOUISIANA

MAINE

QUIZ #8

LESSON 8.4

Identify these states.

1	*ALASKA*	2	*HAWAII*	3	*IDAHO*
4	*CALIFORNIA*	5	*ARIZONA*	6	*COLORADO*
7	*KANSAS*	8	*ARKANSAS*	9	*LOUISIANA*

Identify these states.

1	*IOWA*	2	*ILLINOIS*	3	*INDIANA*
4	*KENTUCKY*	5	*MAINE*	6	*MASSACHUSETTS*
7	*CONNECTICUT*	8	*DELAWARE*	9	*MARYLAND*

STOP

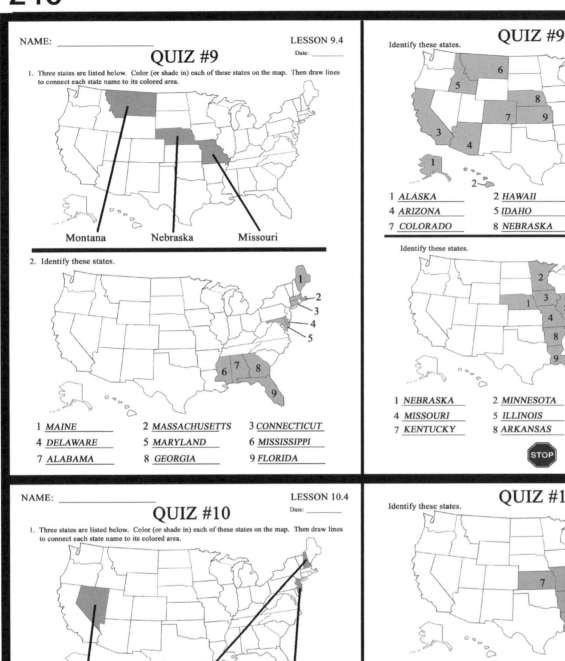

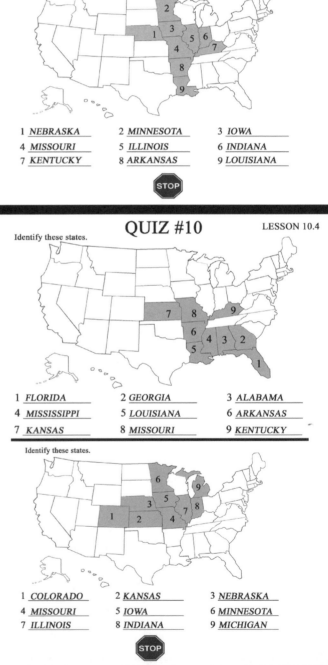

QUIZ #9 — LESSON 9.4

NAME: _____

Date: _____

1. Three states are listed below. Color (or shade in) each of these states on the map. Then draw lines to connect each state name to its colored area.

Montana   Nebraska   Missouri

2. Identify these states.

1 MAINE   2 MASSACHUSETTS   3 CONNECTICUT
4 DELAWARE   5 MARYLAND   6 MISSISSIPPI
7 ALABAMA   8 GEORGIA   9 FLORIDA

QUIZ #9 — LESSON 9.4

Identify these states.

1 ALASKA   2 HAWAII   3 CALIFORNIA
4 ARIZONA   5 IDAHO   6 MONTANA
7 COLORADO   8 NEBRASKA   9 KANSAS

Identify these states.

1 NEBRASKA   2 MINNESOTA   3 IOWA
4 MISSOURI   5 ILLINOIS   6 INDIANA
7 KENTUCKY   8 ARKANSAS   9 LOUISIANA

STOP

QUIZ #10 — LESSON 10.4

NAME: _____

Date: _____

1. Three states are listed below. Color (or shade in) each of these states on the map. Then draw lines to connect each state name to its colored area.

Nevada   New Hampshire   New Jersey

2. Identify these states.

1 MICHIGAN   2 INDIANA   3 MAINE
4 NEW HAMPSHIRE   5 MASSACHUSETTS   6 CONNECTICUT
7 NEW JERSEY   8 DELAWARE   9 MARYLAND

QUIZ #10 — LESSON 10.4

Identify these states.

1 FLORIDA   2 GEORGIA   3 ALABAMA
4 MISSISSIPPI   5 LOUISIANA   6 ARKANSAS
7 KANSAS   8 MISSOURI   9 KENTUCKY

Identify these states.

1 COLORADO   2 KANSAS   3 NEBRASKA
4 MISSOURI   5 IOWA   6 MINNESOTA
7 ILLINOIS   8 INDIANA   9 MICHIGAN

STOP

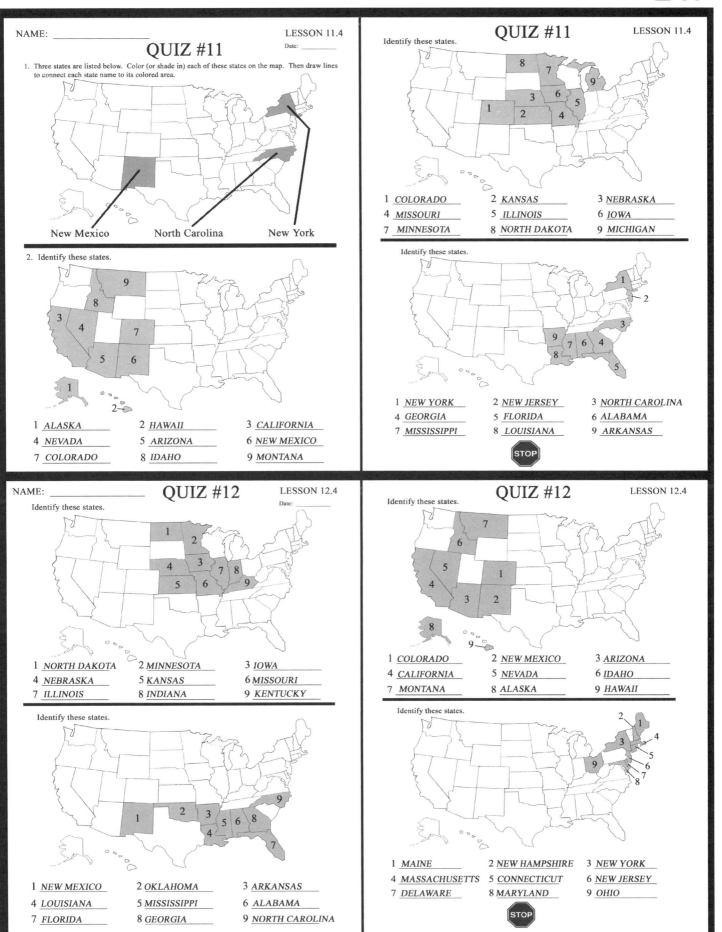

NAME: _____ **QUIZ #11** LESSON 11.4 Date: _____

1. Three states are listed below. Color (or shade in) each of these states on the map. Then draw lines to connect each state name to its colored area.

New Mexico   North Carolina   New York

2. Identify these states.

1 ALASKA	2 HAWAII	3 CALIFORNIA
4 NEVADA	5 ARIZONA	6 NEW MEXICO
7 COLORADO	8 IDAHO	9 MONTANA

QUIZ #11 LESSON 11.4

Identify these states.

1 COLORADO	2 KANSAS	3 NEBRASKA
4 MISSOURI	5 ILLINOIS	6 IOWA
7 MINNESOTA	8 NORTH DAKOTA	9 MICHIGAN

Identify these states.

1 NEW YORK	2 NEW JERSEY	3 NORTH CAROLINA
4 GEORGIA	5 FLORIDA	6 ALABAMA
7 MISSISSIPPI	8 LOUISIANA	9 ARKANSAS

STOP

NAME: _____ **QUIZ #12** LESSON 12.4 Date: _____

Identify these states.

1 NORTH DAKOTA	2 MINNESOTA	3 IOWA
4 NEBRASKA	5 KANSAS	6 MISSOURI
7 ILLINOIS	8 INDIANA	9 KENTUCKY

Identify these states.

1 NEW MEXICO	2 OKLAHOMA	3 ARKANSAS
4 LOUISIANA	5 MISSISSIPPI	6 ALABAMA
7 FLORIDA	8 GEORGIA	9 NORTH CAROLINA

QUIZ #12 LESSON 12.4

Identify these states.

1 COLORADO	2 NEW MEXICO	3 ARIZONA
4 CALIFORNIA	5 NEVADA	6 IDAHO
7 MONTANA	8 ALASKA	9 HAWAII

Identify these states.

1 MAINE	2 NEW HAMPSHIRE	3 NEW YORK
4 MASSACHUSETTS	5 CONNECTICUT	6 NEW JERSEY
7 DELAWARE	8 MARYLAND	9 OHIO

STOP

248

ANSWER KEY

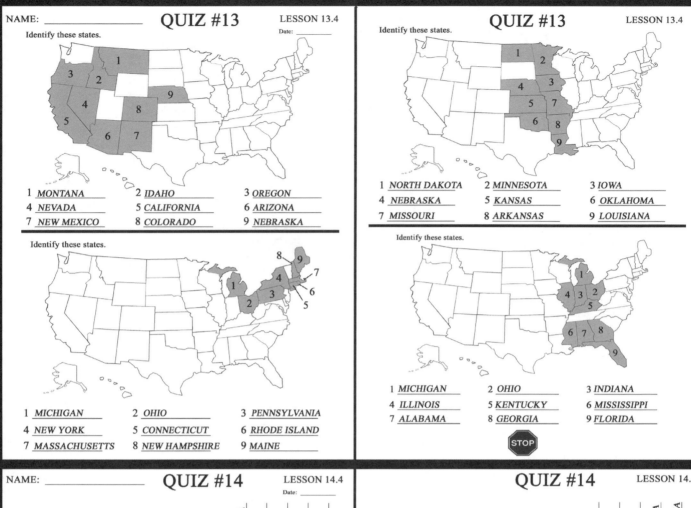

QUIZ #13 — LESSON 13.4

NAME: _____ Date: _____

Identify these states.

1	MONTANA	2	IDAHO	3	OREGON
4	NEVADA	5	CALIFORNIA	6	ARIZONA
7	NEW MEXICO	8	COLORADO	9	NEBRASKA

Identify these states.

1	MICHIGAN	2	OHIO	3	PENNSYLVANIA
4	NEW YORK	5	CONNECTICUT	6	RHODE ISLAND
7	MASSACHUSETTS	8	NEW HAMPSHIRE	9	MAINE

QUIZ #13 — LESSON 13.4

Identify these states.

1	NORTH DAKOTA	2	MINNESOTA	3	IOWA
4	NEBRASKA	5	KANSAS	6	OKLAHOMA
7	MISSOURI	8	ARKANSAS	9	LOUISIANA

Identify these states.

1	MICHIGAN	2	OHIO	3	INDIANA
4	ILLINOIS	5	KENTUCKY	6	MISSISSIPPI
7	ALABAMA	8	GEORGIA	9	FLORIDA

STOP

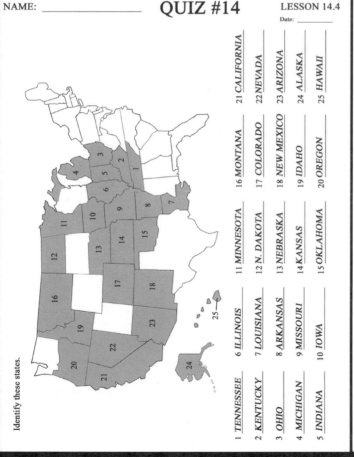

NAME: _____ **QUIZ #14** — LESSON 14.4 Date: _____

Identify these states.

21 CALIFORNIA
22 NEVADA
23 ARIZONA
24 ALASKA
25 HAWAII

16 MONTANA
17 COLORADO
18 NEW MEXICO
19 IDAHO
20 OREGON

11 MINNESOTA
12 N. DAKOTA
13 NEBRASKA
14 KANSAS
15 OKLAHOMA

6 ILLINOIS
7 LOUISIANA
8 ARKANSAS
9 MISSOURI
10 IOWA

1 TENNESSEE
2 KENTUCKY
3 OHIO
4 MICHIGAN
5 INDIANA

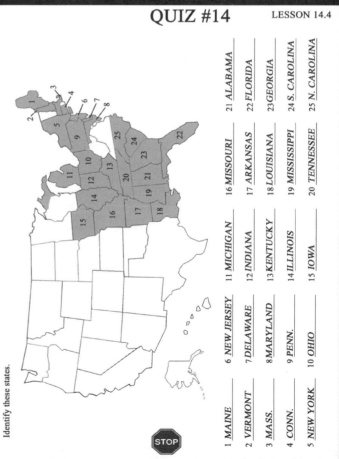

QUIZ #14 — LESSON 14.4

Identify these states.

21 ALABAMA
22 FLORIDA
23 GEORGIA
24 S. CAROLINA
25 N. CAROLINA

16 MISSOURI
17 ARKANSAS
18 LOUISIANA
19 MISSISSIPPI
20 TENNESSEE

11 MICHIGAN
12 INDIANA
13 KENTUCKY
14 ILLINOIS
15 IOWA

6 NEW JERSEY
7 DELAWARE
8 MARYLAND
9 PENN.
10 OHIO

1 MAINE
2 VERMONT
3 MASS.
4 CONN.
5 NEW YORK

STOP

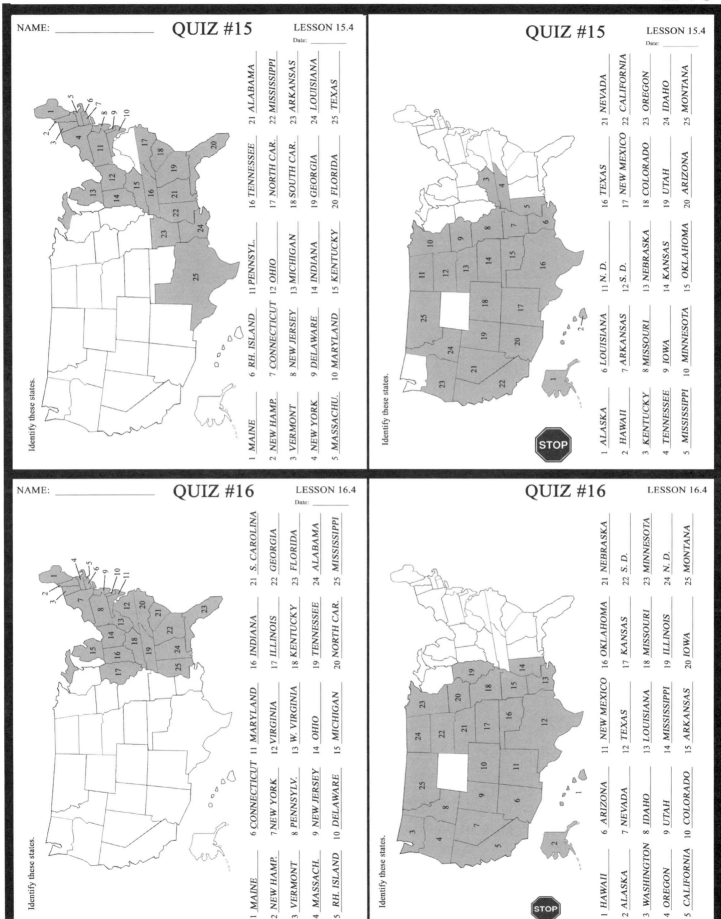

QUIZ #15 — LESSON 15.4

NAME: _____ Date: _____

Identify these states.

1 *MAINE*
2 *NEW HAMP.*
3 *VERMONT*
4 *NEW YORK*
5 *MASSACHU.*

6 *RH. ISLAND*
7 *CONNECTICUT*
8 *NEW JERSEY*
9 *DELAWARE*
10 *MARYLAND*

11 *PENNSYL.*
12 *OHIO*
13 *MICHIGAN*
14 *INDIANA*
15 *KENTUCKY*

16 *TENNESSEE*
17 *NORTH CAR.*
18 *SOUTH CAR.*
19 *GEORGIA*
20 *FLORIDA*

21 *ALABAMA*
22 *MISSISSIPPI*
23 *ARKANSAS*
24 *LOUISIANA*
25 *TEXAS*

QUIZ #15 — LESSON 15.4

NAME: _____ Date: _____

Identify these states.

1 *ALASKA*
2 *HAWAII*
3 *KENTUCKY*
4 *TENNESSEE*
5 *MISSISSIPPI*

6 *LOUISIANA*
7 *ARKANSAS*
8 *MISSOURI*
9 *IOWA*
10 *MINNESOTA*

11 *N. D.*
12 *S. D.*
13 *NEBRASKA*
14 *KANSAS*
15 *OKLAHOMA*

16 *TEXAS*
17 *NEW MEXICO*
18 *COLORADO*
19 *UTAH*
20 *ARIZONA*

21 *NEVADA*
22 *CALIFORNIA*
23 *OREGON*
24 *IDAHO*
25 *MONTANA*

STOP

QUIZ #16 — LESSON 16.4

NAME: _____ Date: _____

Identify these states.

1 *MAINE*
2 *NEW HAMP.*
3 *VERMONT*
4 *MASSACH.*
5 *RH. ISLAND*

6 *CONNECTICUT*
7 *NEW YORK*
8 *PENNSYLV.*
9 *NEW JERSEY*
10 *DELAWARE*

11 *MARYLAND*
12 *VIRGINIA*
13 *W. VIRGINIA*
14 *OHIO*
15 *MICHIGAN*

16 *INDIANA*
17 *ILLINOIS*
18 *KENTUCKY*
19 *TENNESSEE*
20 *NORTH CAR.*

21 *S. CAROLINA*
22 *GEORGIA*
23 *FLORIDA*
24 *ALABAMA*
25 *MISSISSIPPI*

QUIZ #16 — LESSON 16.4

NAME: _____ Date: _____

Identify these states.

1 *HAWAII*
2 *ALASKA*
3 *WASHINGTON*
4 *OREGON*
5 *CALIFORNIA*

6 *ARIZONA*
7 *NEVADA*
8 *IDAHO*
9 *UTAH*
10 *COLORADO*

11 *NEW MEXICO*
12 *TEXAS*
13 *LOUISIANA*
14 *MISSISSIPPI*
15 *ARKANSAS*

16 *OKLAHOMA*
17 *KANSAS*
18 *MISSOURI*
19 *ILLINOIS*
20 *IOWA*

21 *NEBRASKA*
22 *S. D.*
23 *MINNESOTA*
24 *N. D.*
25 *MONTANA*

STOP

250

ANSWER KEY

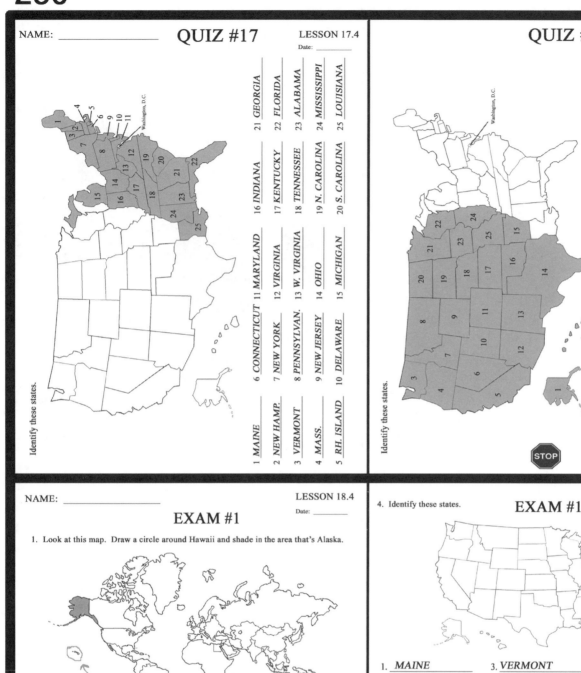

QUIZ #17 — LESSON 17.4

NAME: _____ Date: _____

Identify these states.

1 MAINE
2 NEW HAMP.
3 VERMONT
4 MASS.
5 RH. ISLAND

6 CONNECTICUT
7 NEW YORK
8 PENNSYLVAN.
9 NEW JERSEY
10 DELAWARE

11 MARYLAND
12 VIRGINIA
13 W. VIRGINIA
14 OHIO
15 MICHIGAN

16 INDIANA
17 KENTUCKY
18 TENNESSEE
19 N. CAROLINA
20 S. CAROLINA

21 GEORGIA
22 FLORIDA
23 ALABAMA
24 MISSISSIPPI
25 LOUISIANA

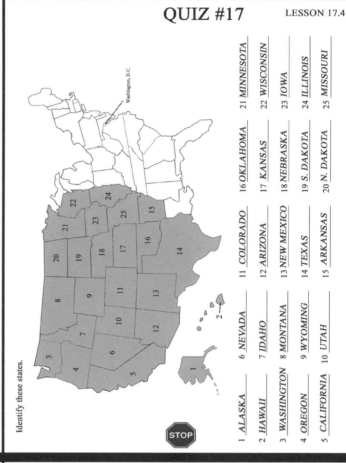

QUIZ #17 — LESSON 17.4

Identify these states.

1 ALASKA
2 HAWAII
3 WASHINGTON
4 OREGON
5 CALIFORNIA

6 NEVADA
7 IDAHO
8 MONTANA
9 WYOMING
10 UTAH

11 COLORADO
12 ARIZONA
13 NEW MEXICO
14 TEXAS
15 ARKANSAS

16 OKLAHOMA
17 KANSAS
18 NEBRASKA
19 S. DAKOTA
20 N. DAKOTA

21 MINNESOTA
22 WISCONSIN
23 IOWA
24 ILLINOIS
25 MISSOURI

STOP

EXAM #1 — LESSON 18.4

NAME: _____ Date: _____

1. Look at this map. Draw a circle around Hawaii and shade in the area that's Alaska.

2. Draw lines to connect each state name to its picture.

Maryland
Rhode Island
Wyoming
Texas
California
Mississippi
Alabama
Delaware

3. Identify these state pictures.

Oklahoma

Connecticut

Utah

Massachusetts

4. Identify these states.

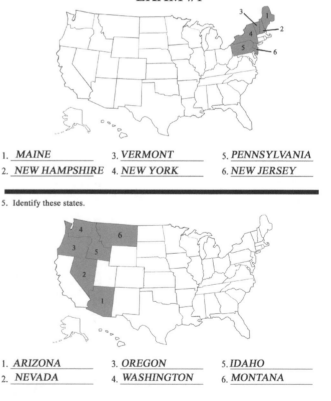

1. *MAINE*
2. *NEW HAMPSHIRE*
3. *VERMONT*
4. *NEW YORK*
5. *PENNSYLVANIA*
6. *NEW JERSEY*

5. Identify these states.

1. *ARIZONA*
2. *NEVADA*
3. *OREGON*
4. *WASHINGTON*
5. *IDAHO*
6. *MONTANA*

(CONTINUE ON NEXT PAGE!)

EXAM #1   LESSON 18.4

6. Identify these states.

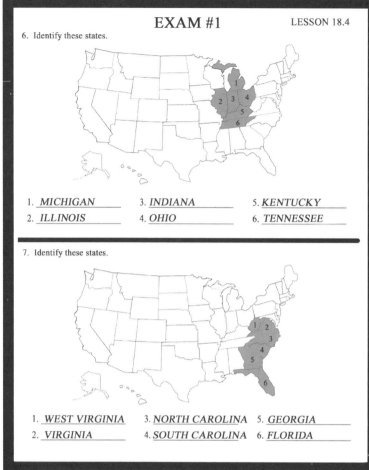

1. *MICHIGAN*   3. *INDIANA*   5. *KENTUCKY*
2. *ILLINOIS*   4. *OHIO*   6. *TENNESSEE*

7. Identify these states.

1. *WEST VIRGINIA*   3. *NORTH CAROLINA*   5. *GEORGIA*
2. *VIRGINIA*   4. *SOUTH CAROLINA*   6. *FLORIDA*

EXAM #1   LESSON 18.4

8. Identify these states.

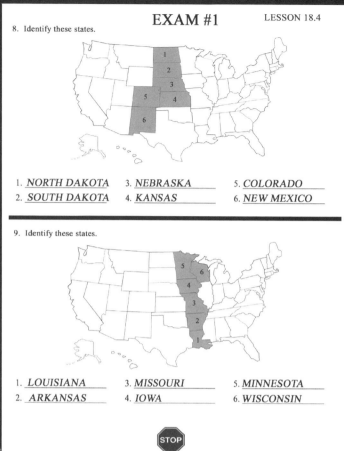

1. *NORTH DAKOTA*   3. *NEBRASKA*   5. *COLORADO*
2. *SOUTH DAKOTA*   4. *KANSAS*   6. *NEW MEXICO*

9. Identify these states.

1. *LOUISIANA*   3. *MISSOURI*   5. *MINNESOTA*
2. *ARKANSAS*   4. *IOWA*   6. *WISCONSIN*

STOP

THIS IS THE END OF THE FIRST SEMESTER'S LESSONS

QUIZ #19

NAME: _____

LESSON 19.4

Date: _____

1. Draw lines to connect each capital city to its home state.

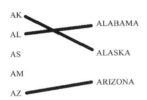

MONTGOMERY   ARIZONA
PHOENIX   ALABAMA
JUNEAU   ALASKA

2. Draw lines to connect each state to the correct abbreviation. Some of the abbreviations won't be used.

AK
AL
AS
AM
AZ

ALABAMA
ALASKA
ARIZONA

3. Do not use a map. In each box below, there is a state that is underlined. Beneath that state, four other states are listed. Of these four states, cross out the ones that DO NOT share a border with the underlined state.

ARIZONA	ALASKA	ALABAMA
NEW MEXICO	~~NEW MEXICO~~	TENNESSEE
UTAH	~~ARIZONA~~	GEORGIA
CALIFORNIA	~~CALIFORNIA~~	FLORIDA
~~FLORIDA~~	~~ALABAMA~~	~~OKLAHOMA~~

STOP

QUIZ #20

NAME: _____

LESSON 20.4

Date: _____

1. Draw lines to connect each capital city to its home state.

LITTLE ROCK   CALIFORNIA
DENVER   ARKANSAS
SACRAMENTO   COLORADO

2. Draw lines to connect each state to the correct abbreviation. Some of the abbreviations won't be used.

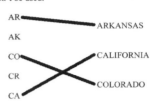

AR
AK
CO
CR
CA

ARKANSAS
CALIFORNIA
COLORADO

3. Do not use a map. In each box below, there is a state that is underlined. Beneath that state, four other states are listed. Of these four states, cross out the ones that DO NOT share a border with the underlined state.

ARKANSAS	CALIFORNIA	COLORADO
~~ALASKA~~	OREGON	WYOMING
TENNESSEE	~~WASHINGTON~~	NEW MEXICO
MISSISSIPPI	NEVADA	~~IOWA~~
TEXAS	ARIZONA	~~KENTUCKY~~

STOP

QUIZ #21

NAME: _____

LESSON 21.4

Date: _____

1. Draw lines to connect each capital city to its home state.

HARTFORD   FLORIDA
TALLAHASSEE   CONNECTICUT
DOVER   DELAWARE

2. Draw lines to connect each state to the correct abbreviation. Some of the abbreviations won't be used.

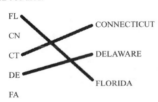

FL
CN
CT
DE
FA

CONNECTICUT
DELAWARE
FLORIDA

3. Do not use a map. In each box below, there is a state that is underlined. Beneath that state, four other states are listed. Of these four states, cross out the ones that DO NOT share a border with the underlined state.

CONNECTICUT	DELAWARE	FLORIDA
NEW YORK	MARYLAND	~~NORTH CAROLINA~~
RHODE ISLAND	PENNSYLVANIA	~~SOUTH CAROLINA~~
~~MAINE~~	NEW JERSEY	GEORGIA
MASSACHUSETTS	~~RHODE ISLAND~~	ALABAMA

QUIZ #22

NAME: _____

LESSON 22.4

Date: _____

1. Draw lines to connect each capital city to its home state.

ATLANTA   GEORGIA
BOISE   HAWAII
HONOLULU   IDAHO

2. Draw lines to connect each state to the correct abbreviation. Some of the abbreviations won't be used.

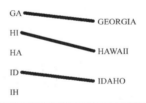

GA
HI
HA
ID
IH

GEORGIA
HAWAII
IDAHO

3. Do not use a map. In each box below, there is a state that is underlined. Beneath that state, four other states are listed. Of these four states, cross out the ones that DO NOT share a border with the underlined state.

GEORGIA	HAWAII	IDAHO
ALABAMA	~~ALASKA~~	WASHINGTON
~~MISSISSIPPI~~	~~CALIFORNIA~~	OREGON
FLORIDA	~~WASHINGTON~~	MONTANA
TENNESSEE	~~GEORGIA~~	~~NORTH DAKOTA~~

STOP

QUIZ #23
NAME: _____ Date: _____

1. Draw lines to connect each capital city to its home state.

INDIANAPOLIS — ILLINOIS
DES MOINES — INDIANA
SPRINGFIELD — IOWA

2. Draw lines to connect each state to the correct abbreviation. Some of the abbreviations won't be used.

IN — ILLINOIS
IA
ID — INDIANA
IL
IW — IOWA

3. Do not use a map. In each box below, there is a state that is underlined. Beneath that state, four other states are listed. Of these four states, cross out the ones that DO NOT share a border with the underlined state.

ILLINOIS	INDIANA	IOWA
INDIANA	MICHIGAN	~~NORTH DAKOTA~~
KENTUCKY	~~PENNSYLVANIA~~	SOUTH DAKOTA
MISSOURI	~~NEW YORK~~	NEBRASKA
~~WEST VIRGINIA~~	OHIO	WISCONSIN

STOP

QUIZ #24
LESSON 24.4
NAME: _____ Date: _____

1. Draw lines to connect each capital city to its home state.

TOPEKA — KANSAS
FRANKFORT — KENTUCKY
BATON ROUGE — LOUISIANA

2. Draw lines to connect each state to the correct abbreviation. Some of the abbreviations won't be used.

LA — KANSAS
KT
KS — KENTUCKY
KY
LO — LOUISIANA

3. Do not use a map. In each box below, there is a state that is underlined. Beneath that state, four other states are listed. Of these four states, cross out the ones that DO NOT share a border with the underlined state.

KANSAS	KENTUCKY	LOUISIANA
OKLAHOMA	WEST VIRGINIA	~~NEW MEXICO~~
~~TEXAS~~	VIRGINIA	TEXAS
COLORADO	OHIO	MISSISSIPPI
MISSOURI	~~PENNSYLVANIA~~	ARKANSAS

STOP

QUIZ #25
LESSON 25.4
NAME: _____ Date: _____

1. Draw lines to connect each capital city to its home state.

BOSTON — MAINE
AUGUSTA — MARYLAND
ANNAPOLIS — MASSACHUSETTS

2. Draw lines to connect each state to the correct abbreviation. Some of the abbreviations won't be used.

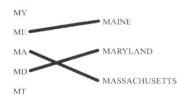

MY — MAINE
ME
MA — MARYLAND
MD
MT — MASSACHUSETTS

3. Do not use a map. In each box below, there is a state that is underlined. Beneath that state, four other states are listed. Of these four states, cross out the ones that DO NOT share a border with the underlined state.

MAINE	MARYLAND	MASSACHUSETTS
~~NEW YORK~~	VIRGINIA	RHODE ISLAND
NEW HAMPSHIRE	DELAWARE	VERMONT
~~PENNSYLVANIA~~	~~NEW YORK~~	NEW YORK
~~MARYLAND~~	WEST VIRGINIA	~~PENNSYLVANIA~~

STOP

QUIZ #26
LESSON 26.4
NAME: _____ Date: _____

1. Draw lines to connect each capital city to its home state.

SAINT PAUL — MICHIGAN
JACKSON — MINNESOTA
LANSING — MISSISSIPPI

2. Draw lines to connect each state to the correct abbreviation. Some of the abbreviations won't be used.

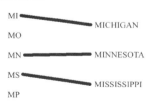

MI — MICHIGAN
MO
MN — MINNESOTA
MS — MISSISSIPPI
MP

3. Do not use a map. In each box below, there is a state that is underlined. Beneath that state, four other states are listed. Of these four states, cross out the ones that DO NOT share a border with the underlined state.

MICHIGAN	MINNESOTA	MISSISSIPPI
OHIO	NORTH DAKOTA	~~TEXAS~~
INDIANA	SOUTH DAKOTA	LOUISIANA
WISCONSIN	~~MISSOURI~~	ARKANSAS
~~KENTUCKY~~	IOWA	ALABAMA

STOP

QUIZ #27

NAME: _____   LESSON 27.4
                               Date: _____

1. Draw lines to connect each capital city to its home state.

HELENA   MISSOURI
LINCOLN   MONTANA
JEFFERSON CITY NEBRASKA

2. Draw lines to connect each state to the correct abbreviation. Some of the abbreviations won't be used.

MO
MT   MISSOURI
MA   MONTANA
NB
NE   NEBRASKA

3. Do not use a map. In each box below, there is a state that is underlined. Beneath that state, four other states are listed. Of these four states, cross out the ones that DO NOT share a border with the underlined state.

MISSOURI	MONTANA	NEBRASKA
~~WEST VIRGINIA~~	NORTH DAKOTA	~~NORTH DAKOTA~~
KENTUCKY	SOUTH DAKOTA	SOUTH DAKOTA
ARKANSAS	~~WASHINGTON~~	IOWA
~~LOUISIANA~~	IDAHO	KANSAS

STOP

QUIZ #28

NAME: _____   LESSON 28.4
                               Date: _____

1. Draw lines to connect each capital city to its home state.

CONCORD   NEVADA
CARSON CITY   NEW HAMPSHIRE
TRENTON   NEW JERSEY

2. Draw lines to connect each state to the correct abbreviation. Some of the abbreviations won't be used.

NH
NJ   NEVADA
NA   NEW HAMPSHIRE
NP
NV   NEW JERSEY

3. Do not use a map. In each box below, there is a state that is underlined. Beneath that state, four other states are listed. Of these four states, cross out the ones that DO NOT share a border with the underlined state.

NEVADA	NEW HAMPSHIRE	NEW JERSEY
OREGON	~~NEW YORK~~	NEW YORK
CALIFORNIA	~~NEW JERSEY~~	PENNSYLVANIA
~~OKLAHOMA~~	MAINE	~~VIRGINIA~~
ARIZONA	~~NEW MEXICO~~	~~WEST VIRGINIA~~

STOP

QUIZ #29

NAME: _____   LESSON 29.4
                               Date: _____

1. Draw lines to connect each capital city to its home state.

ALBANY   NEW MEXICO
RALEIGH   NEW YORK
SANTA FE   NORTH CAROLINA

2. Draw lines to connect each state to the correct abbreviation. Some of the abbreviations won't be used.

NO
NY   NEW MEXICO
NC   NEW YORK
NE
NM   NORTH CAROLINA

3. Do not use a map. In each box below, there is a state that is underlined. Beneath that state, four other states are listed. Of these four states, cross out the ones that DO NOT share a border with the underlined state.

NEW MEXICO	NEW YORK	NORTH CAROLINA
TEXAS	NEW JERSEY	SOUTH CAROLINA
ARIZONA	PENNSYLVANIA	~~FLORIDA~~
OKLAHOMA	~~WEST VIRGINIA~~	VIRGINIA
~~CALIFORNIA~~	~~CALIFORNIA~~	TENNESSEE

STOP

QUIZ #30

NAME: _____   LESSON 30.4
                               Date: _____

1. Draw lines to connect each capital city to its home state.

OKLAHOMA CITY   NORTH DAKOTA
BISMARCK   OHIO
COLUMBUS   OKLAHOMA

2. Draw lines to connect each state to the correct abbreviation. Some of the abbreviations won't be used.

NK
ND   NORTH DAKOTA
OK   OHIO
OI
OH   OKLAHOMA

3. Do not use a map. In each box below, there is a state that is underlined. Beneath that state, four other states are listed. Of these four states, cross out the ones that DO NOT share a border with the underlined state.

NORTH DAKOTA	OHIO	OKLAHOMA
MONTANA	PENNSYLVANIA	~~CALIFORNIA~~
SOUTH DAKOTA	MICHIGAN	~~LOUISIANA~~
~~MICHIGAN~~	WEST VIRGINIA	TEXAS
~~OREGON~~	~~VIRGINIA~~	ARKANSAS

STOP

QUIZ #31

NAME: _____   LESSON 31.4

Date: _____

1. Draw lines to connect each capital city to its home state.

HARRISBURG — OREGON
SALEM — PENNSYLVANIA
PROVIDENCE — RHODE ISLAND

2. Draw lines to connect each state to the correct abbreviation. Some of the abbreviations won't be used.

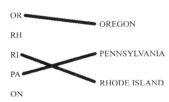

OR — OREGON
RH
RI — PENNSYLVANIA
PA — RHODE ISLAND
ON

3. Do not use a map. In each box below, there is a state that is underlined. Beneath that state, four other states are listed. Of these four states, cross out the ones that <u>DO NOT</u> share a border with the underlined state.

OREGON	PENNSYLVANIA	RHODE ISLAND
CALIFORNIA	NEW YORK	MASSACHUSETTS
WASHINGTON	OHIO	~~MAINE~~
IDAHO	~~MAINE~~	CONNECTICUT
~~ARIZONA~~	MARYLAND	~~MARYLAND~~

STOP

QUIZ #32

NAME: _____   LESSON 32.4

Date: _____

1. Draw lines to connect each capital city to its home state.

COLUMBIA — SOUTH CAROLINA
NASHVILLE — SOUTH DAKOTA
PIERRE — TENNESSEE

2. Draw lines to connect each state to the correct abbreviation. Some of the abbreviations won't be used.

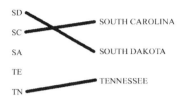

SD — SOUTH CAROLINA
SC
SA — SOUTH DAKOTA
TE
TN — TENNESSEE

3. Do not use a map. In each box below, there is a state that is underlined. Beneath that state, four other states are listed. Of these four states, cross out the ones that <u>DO NOT</u> share a border with the underlined state.

SOUTH CAROLINA	SOUTH DAKOTA	TENNESSEE
NORTH CAROLINA	~~MICHIGAN~~	KENTUCKY
~~VIRGINIA~~	NORTH DAKOTA	VIRGINIA
GEORGIA	MINNESOTA	NORTH CAROLINA
~~LOUISIANA~~	MONTANA	~~SOUTH CAROLINA~~

STOP

QUIZ #33

NAME: _____   LESSON 33.4

Date: _____

1. Draw lines to connect each capital city to its home state.

SALT LAKE CITY — TEXAS
AUSTIN — UTAH
MONTPELIER — VERMONT

2. Draw lines to connect each state to the correct abbreviation. Some of the abbreviations won't be used.

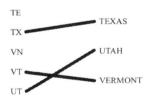

TE — TEXAS
TX
VN — UTAH
VT
UT — VERMONT

3. Do not use a map. In each box below, there is a state that is underlined. Beneath that state, four other states are listed. Of these four states, cross out the ones that <u>DO NOT</u> share a border with the underlined state.

TEXAS	UTAH	VERMONT
LOUISIANA	IDAHO	NEW YORK
OKLAHOMA	~~NORTH DAKOTA~~	NEW HAMPSHIRE
NEW MEXICO	~~WASHINGTON~~	MASSACHUSETTS
~~ARIZONA~~	COLORADO	~~MAINE~~

STOP

QUIZ #34

NAME: _____   LESSON 34.4

Date: _____

1. Draw lines to connect each capital city to its home state.

RICHMOND — VIRGINIA
CHARLESTON — WASHINGTON
OLYMPIA — WEST VIRGINIA

2. Draw lines to connect each state to the correct abbreviation. Some of the abbreviations won't be used.

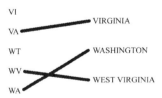

VI — VIRGINIA
VA
WT — WASHINGTON
WV — WEST VIRGINIA
WA

3. Do not use a map. In each box below, there is a state that is underlined. Beneath that state, four other states are listed. Of these four states, cross out the ones that <u>DO NOT</u> share a border with the underlined state.

VIRGINIA	WASHINGTON	WEST VIRGINIA
MARYLAND	~~ALASKA~~	OHIO
WEST VIRGINIA	OREGON	KENTUCKY
NORTH CAROLINA	~~CALIFORNIA~~	VIRGINIA
~~SOUTH CAROLINA~~	IDAHO	~~ILLINOIS~~

STOP

256

ANSWER KEY

NAME: _____

LESSON 35.4

QUIZ #35

Date: _____

1. Draw lines to connect each capital city to its home state.

MADISON ━━━━━━━ WISCONSIN

CHEYENNE ━━━━━━━ WYOMING

2. Draw lines to connect each state to the correct abbreviation. Some of the abbreviations won't be used.

WI

WN ━━━━━━━ WISCONSIN

WO ━━━━━━━ WYOMING

WY

3. Do not use a map. In each box below, there is a state that is underlined. Beneath that state, four other states are listed. Of these four states, cross out the ones that DO NOT share a border with the underlined state.

WISCONSIN	WYOMING
MICHIGAN	COLORADO
~~NEW YORK~~	MONTANA
~~KENTUCKY~~	~~WASHINGTON~~
ILLINOIS	~~TEXAS~~

4. Washington, D.C. borders two states. Name them. __MARYLAND__ and __VIRGINIA__.

(STOP)

EXAM #2

LESSON 36.4

1. Fill in the blanks with the correct state abbreviations.

AL Alabama	**LA** Louisiana	**OH** Ohio
AK Alaska	**ME** Maine	**OK** Oklahoma
AZ Arizona	**MD** Maryland	**OR** Oregon
AK Arkansas	**MA** Massachusetts	**PA** Pennsylvania
CA California	**MI** Michigan	**RI** Rhode Island
CO Colorado	**MN** Minnesota	**SC** South Carolina
CT Connecticut	**MS** Mississippi	**SD** South Dakota
DE Delaware	**MO** Missouri	**TN** Tennessee
FL Florida	**MT** Montana	**TX** Texas
GA Georgia	**NE** Nebraska	**UT** Utah
HI Hawaii	**NV** Nevada	**VT** Vermont
ID Idaho	**NH** New Hampshire	**VA** Virginia
IL Illinois	**NJ** New Jersey	**WA** Washington
IN Indiana	**NM** New Mexico	**WV** West Virginia
IA Iowa	**NY** New York	**WI** Wisconsin
KS Kansas	**NC** North Carolina	**WY** Wyoming
KY Kentucky	**ND** North Dakota	

2. What is the abbreviation for Washington, D.C.? __DC__

3. What two states border Washington, D.C.? __MARYLAND__ and __VIRGINIA__.

4. What is the capital of The United States of America? __WASHINGTON, D.C.__

5. The United States is made up of how many states? __50__

EXAM #2

LESSON 36.4

6. Match each capital to its state.

H Alaska		A. Frankfort
E California		B. Madison
J Delaware		C. Columbus
G Hawaii		D. Providence
O Illinois		E. Sacramento
A Kentucky		F. Trenton
I Louisiana		G. Honolulu
M Minnesota		H. Juneau
F New Jersey		I. Baton Rouge
K North Dakota		J. Dover
C Ohio		K. Bismarck
D Rhode Island		L. Austin
L Texas		M. Saint Paul
N Washington		N. Olympia
B Wisconsin		O. Springfield

EXAM #2

LESSON 36.4

7. In each box, there are some states. These states share a border with one other state. Write the name of that state on the blank line in the box.

CALIFORNIA	PENNSYLVANIA	GEORGIA
OREGON	NEW YORK	ALABAMA
NEVADA	MARYLAND	FLORIDA
ARIZONA	OHIO	NORTH CAROLINA
	WEST VIRGINIA	SOUTH CAROLINA

OKLAHOMA	NEBRASKA	TENNESSEE
TEXAS	WYOMING	KENTUCKY
COLORADO	COLORADO	NORTH CAROLINA
MISSOURI	IOWA	ALABAMA
ARKANSAS	MISSOURI	ARKANSAS

MASSACHUSETTS	WISCONSIN	MISSOURI
CONNECTICUT	MINNESOTA	ILLINOIS
RHODE ISLAND	MICHIGAN	TENNESSEE
NEW YORK	IOWA	ARKANSAS
NEW HAMPSHIRE	ILLINOIS	KANSAS

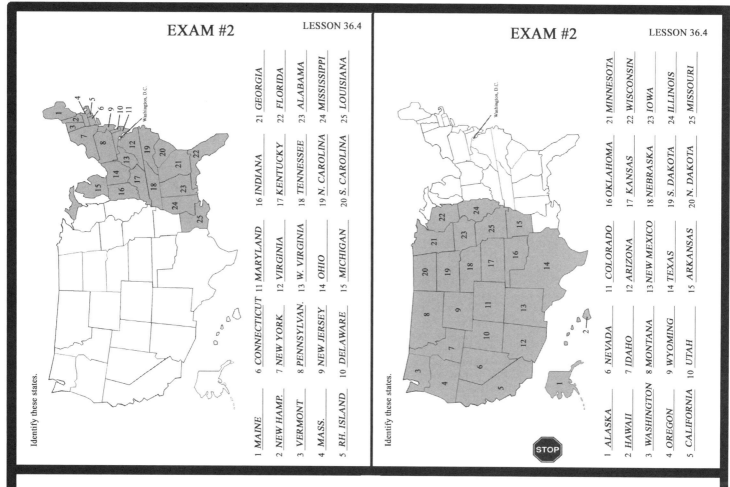

EXAM #2   LESSON 36.4

Identify these states.

1 *MAINE*
2 *NEW HAMP.*
3 *VERMONT*
4 *MASS.*
5 *RH. ISLAND*

6 *CONNECTICUT*
7 *NEW YORK*
8 *PENNSYLVAN.*
9 *NEW JERSEY*
10 *DELAWARE*

11 *MARYLAND*
12 *VIRGINIA*
13 *W. VIRGINIA*
14 *OHIO*
15 *MICHIGAN*

16 *INDIANA*
17 *KENTUCKY*
18 *TENNESSEE*
19 *N. CAROLINA*
20 *S. CAROLINA*

21 *GEORGIA*
22 *FLORIDA*
23 *ALABAMA*
24 *MISSISSIPPI*
25 *LOUISIANA*

EXAM #2   LESSON 36.4

Identify these states.

1 *ALASKA*
2 *HAWAII*
3 *WASHINGTON*
4 *OREGON*
5 *CALIFORNIA*

6 *NEVADA*
7 *IDAHO*
8 *MONTANA*
9 *WYOMING*
10 *UTAH*

11 *COLORADO*
12 *ARIZONA*
13 *NEW MEXICO*
14 *TEXAS*
15 *ARKANSAS*

16 *OKLAHOMA*
17 *KANSAS*
18 *NEBRASKA*
19 *S. DAKOTA*
20 *N. DAKOTA*

21 *MINNESOTA*
22 *WISCONSIN*
23 *IOWA*
24 *ILLINOIS*
25 *MISSOURI*

STOP

THIS IS THE END OF THE SECOND SEMESTER'S MATERIAL

How to grade the quizzes and exams.

The scoring of quizzes and exams is left to the discretion of the instructor. However, an optional report card has been furnished on the following page to help you keep track of the student's progress. With this optional report card, quizzes can receive a maximum of 10 points and the two exams can receive a maximum of 30 points.

Some suggestions for scoring are as follows, but, again, it is left to your discretion.

QUIZ Scores	# of Mistakes
10/10	0
9/10	1
8/10	2
7/10	3
6/10	4
*	*
*	*
*	*

EXAM Scores	# of Mistakes
30/30	0
29/30	1
28/30	2
27/30	3
26/30	4
*	*
*	*
*	*

STUDENT RECORD

Name: _____   Grade: _____

Subject: __American Geography__   School Year: _____

1ST SEMSTER	
LESSON 1.4 QUIZ #1	__/10
LESSON 2.4 QUIZ #2	__/10
LESSON 3.4 QUIZ #3	__/10
LESSON 4.4 QUIZ #3	__/10
LESSON 5.4 QUIZ #5	__/10
LESSON 6.4 QUIZ #6	__/10
LESSON 7.4 QUIZ #7	__/10
LESSON 8.4 QUIZ #8	__/10
LESSON 9.4 QUIZ #9	__/10
LESSON 10.4 QUIZ #10	__/10
LESSON 11.4 QUIZ #11	__/10
LESSON 12.4 QUIZ #12	__/10
LESSON 13.4 QUIZ #13	__/10
LESSON 14.4 QUIZ #14	__/10
LESSON 15.4 QUIZ #15	__/10
LESSON 16.4 QUIZ #16	__/10
LESSON 17.4 QUIZ #17	__/10
LESSON 18.4 EXAM #1	__/30
SEMESTER SCORE	__/200
SEMESTER GRADE	_____

2ND SEMSTER	
LESSON 19.4 QUIZ #19	__/10
LESSON 20.4 QUIZ #20	__/10
LESSON 21.4 QUIZ #21	__/10
LESSON 22.4 QUIZ #22	__/10
LESSON 23.4 QUIZ #23	__/10
LESSON 24.4 QUIZ #24	__/10
LESSON 25.4 QUIZ #25	__/10
LESSON 26.4 QUIZ #26	__/10
LESSON 27.4 QUIZ #27	__/10
LESSON 28.4 QUIZ #28	__/10
LESSON 29.4 QUIZ #29	__/10
LESSON 30.4 QUIZ #30	__/10
LESSON 31.4 QUIZ #31	__/10
LESSON 32.4 QUIZ #32	__/10
LESSON 33.4 QUIZ #33	__/10
LESSON 34.4 QUIZ #34	__/10
LESSON 35.4 QUIZ #35	__/10
LESSON 36.4 EXAM #2	__/30
SEMESTER SCORE	__/200
SEMESTER GRADE	_____

About the Author:

Joel King is a home school dad with a passion for writing Christian fiction and creating educational resources with unique twists. He loves to play games with his three boys and believes that children retain knowledge better when they are having fun. Joel has a B.S. degree in accounting from the University of Kentucky and works as a state auditor. He lives with his wife and three boys in western Kentucky where they have home schooled their children for six years.

QUICK ORDER FORM

Would you like your own copy of the Star-Spangled State Book and companion Work-book, a 36-week curriculum, chock full of games, puzzles, Þll-in-the-blank exercises and maps? Simply indicate the products that interest you and get in touch with us in one of the ways below.

☐ Star-Spangled State Book (companion book to this one) - $18.95
☐ Star-Spangled Workbook + reproducible CD - $34.95
☐ Or request a free catalog and sampler CD which contains samples and entire ebooks which represent our line of quality history and geography resources meant to educate and entertain your students.

Fax Orders: Fax this form to (210)568-9655
Telephone Orders: Call 1(877)697-8611 toll free with your credit card in hand
Mail Orders: Send this form to:

Knowledge Quest, Inc.
4210 Misty Glade, Ste B
San Antonio, TX 78247
(210)745-0203

Name: ——————————————————————————

Address: ——————————————————————————

City: ——————————————————————————

State: ——————————————————————————

Zip: ——————————————————————————

Telephone: ——————————————————————————

Email: ——————————————————————————

Subtotal for books indicated above: ——————————
US Shipping, please add $5 for single title and $2 for additional title: ——————————
Total amount enclosed: ——————————

Payment:

☐ check
☐ credit card (indicate type)

Card number: ——————————————————————————

Name on card: ——————————————————————————

Expiration date: ——————————————————————————

Yes, we do sell wholesale as well. Need to contact us about group use? Send an email to orders@knowledgequestmaps.com or visit us online at www.knowledgequestmaps.com